Family Wicca

Revised and Expanded Edition

Practical Paganism
for
Parents and Children

Ashleen O'Gaea

New Page Books
A division of The Career Press, Inc.
Franklin Lakes, NJ

FAMILY WICCA, REVISED AND EXPANDED EDITION
EDITED BY CHRISTOPHER CAROLEI
TYPESET BY EILEEN DOW MUNSON
Cover design by Conker Tree Design
Printed in the U.S.A. by Book-mart Press

To order this title, please call toll-free 1-800-CAREER-1 (NJ and Canada: 201-848-0310) to order using VISA or MasterCard, or for further information on books from Career Press.

The Career Press, Inc., 3 Tice Road, PO Box 687,
Franklin Lakes, NJ 07417
www.careerpress.com
www.newpagebooks.com

Library of Congress Cataloging-in-Publication Data

O'Gaea, Ashleen.
    Family Wicca : practical paganism for parents and children / by Ashleen O'Gaea.—Rev. and expanded ed.
        p. cm.
    Rev. ed. Of: The family Wicca book. 1st ed. 1993.
    Includes bibliographical references and index.
    ISBN-13: 978-1-56414-886-5 (pbk.)
    ISBN-10: 1-56414-886-6 (pbk.)
        1. Witchcraft. 2. Family—Religious life. 3. Child rearing—Religious aspects—Goddess religion. 4. Goddess religion. I. O'Gaea, Ashleen. Family Wicca book. II. Title.

BF1572.F35O35 2006
299'.94--dc22

                                                                    2005058052

Acknowledgments

It's been about 10 years since the first edition of *Family Wicca* came out. It was a long time after that before I published any more books, though I wrote *Raising Witches* and *In the Service of Life* almost immediately afterwards. Those books and this one were revised in light of many experiences, including those involving my local community (TAWN, the Tucson Area Wiccan-Pagan Network).

I owe thanks to the several people who told me that they moved to Tucson because of what they read about TAWN in the first edition of this book, or that they were excited to move here because they knew from *Family Wicca* that there was a strong Neo-Pagan community here. I owe thanks to the people who've told me that they were "thrilled" to meet me, and happy to find out I'm just a regular person, and not one of those intimidating authors. I owe thanks to the few people who've told me the first edition of *Family Wicca* moved them to tears, and to the fair number of people who continue to contact me online to say that *Family Wicca* has been, or is, helpful to them, and those who still occasionally come across it for the first time and review it for their favorite magazine.

I offer thanks, also, to the reviewer (in a now-forgotten venue) who stated that her one problem with *Family Wicca* was that I didn't stress enough that children shouldn't let people touch them improperly. I thought, and still think, that's more of a family thing than a Wicca thing, but her concern probably came from experience, and so I added that emphasis in this edition, and reiterate it here. Kids need to explore the world, yes, and to fall down and get back up. And we parents can't control what happens in their every relationship. But we need to protect them as fiercely as we can from abuse of any kind while they're growing up, and if something happens anyway, make darned sure they know it is just flat-out not their fault.

I also want to thank Isaac Bonewits, who nudged me a couple of times about a second edition of this book.

You can't have a *Family Wicca* book without family. Obviously I couldn't have written either edition without Canyondancer and the Explorer. But I couldn't have written *Family Wicca* without the people I count as my Pagan family: Rock and Heather; Sue, Al, Cait, and Rowie; Don and Arlene; Carol and CJ; Gannd, John, Caryl, and Faerie Moon; Sylvia and her daughters; Isaac; M.R. and his wife and daughter; Grey Cat; Grianwydd; Jacquie and Don; Deliana, Rick, Cerridwen, and Shea; Lisa, Jim, and Skye; Betty; Kerr and Phoenix; Craig, Morgana, Jess, and Deborah; Neil, Alicen, Morgan, and Tam Lin; all of the Campsight Coveners; Patricia and Larry; Alex and Susie; Richard; Nancy and Debra; Sepp and Mary; My dear friend Owl; Patrick and Deborah; Donna, Dave, and Lezli, and the rest of the Sacred Stone People; Phyllis and Beryl; Morgana; Cheryl and her children; Brandyn and her own; Dr. Shelley; the late Roderick Runesayer; Ikari; all of the MEM volunteers; Stan; Bridget; Mark S.; Marc H.; Janet H.; Trish; Tish and "Uncle" Owen; Vasalisa, Murchadh, and Ivy; and Lyon.

That's a long list of names, and it might not be long enough. Whoever I've left out, forgive me: your names are in my heart even if they're not on this page. I've learned something from all of you, and I've felt support from each of you just when I needed it. I can't pay you back for your love and friendship through the years, but I hope to pay it forward, sharing your spirit with those who read this second edition of *Family Wicca*.

Brave heart and bright blessings,
Ashleen O'Gaea
November 2005

Contents

Preface

More than a decade after *Family Wicca* was first published, I still get letters thanking me for writing it, and letting me know that the first edition has made a difference in people's lives. I still see the occasional contemporary review, too, and most of them are still wholly favorable. But 10 -plus years later, it's time for an update.

Not everything has changed, of course, and much that has is different only in detail, and not in general principle. Families are still (even more?) diverse, and Neo-Pagans still want some ideas for sharing and integrating their Paganism with the non-Pagan people and ordinary doings of their lives. But I have updated some rituals, and commented on some of the old material.

There are now other books about Pagan families, and about raising kids in a Pagan family (and I've written some of them myself), but *Family Wicca*'s format and perspective still speaks to sharing and integration. Like other books I've written (with Canyondancer's help, even though his name's not on all the covers), *Family Wicca* emphasizes context and community as much as, if not more than, individual Witchcraft.

This second edition was revised from the small home office that 'dancer and I share. It overlooks the courtyard of our present home. I no longer hear the "bleepity-bleep" of my son's video games, or the boisterous sound tracks of the television shows he enjoyed in his youth. (He's 26 years old now, not the 8-year-old whose smiling face appeared with 'dancer's and mine on the cover of the first edition; he lives in his own house; and he's not Wiccan now.)

But I'm writing this preface on a Thursday, which means it's the night he'll be over at our house for dinner, and we'll be watching a University of Arizona Wildcats basketball game together before he goes home, so instead of video game sounds or laugh tracks I'll be hearing the squeak of athletic shoes on the Lute and Bobbie Olson ball court's polished wooden floor.

Speaking of cats, we live with different house cats than we did when the Explorer was growing up, but the ones we have now will, as the others used to, be swarming us, and the dog we got a few years after the publication of *Family Wicca* will be on the couch snuggling with the Explorer. It's a "different-but-the-same" homey scene, and just as heartwarming.

Families change, and yet remain families, just as children grow up, yet remain our children. Wicca changes as well, as does/should our understanding and practice of it as we mature. Please consider this second edition of *Family Wicca* our salute to the growth of our son, your kids, our families and communities, and Wicca.

Introduction

The *Family Wicca Book* was published in 1993, and *Family Wicca* is, in 2006, about society, history, magic, psychology, politics, ritual, education, changing the world, and Wiccan families. Why are these subjects all in the same book? Because children grow up in families, families emerge from social groups, social groups exist within societies, and societies both create and are created by their cultures. And cultures are historical, magical, political, and so on.

The foundations of our social institutions are patriarchal, monotheistic assumptions based on the premise that, unless we are forcibly restrained, humans will do horrible things to each other. All the evidence of prepatriarchal primal cultures shows that the first humans were cooperative and gentle with each other, caring for their aged and infirm, and *not* living as movies like *2001* would imply.

There is evidence, too, of sophisticated religious beliefs that included an understanding of the grave as womb: we have found in Shanidar IV, a burial site in a cave in what is now Iraq, pollen (now fossilized) sprinkled over the dead who were carefully restored, some 60,000 years ago, to the fetal position for burial.

And what has any of this to do with children? Just about everything! In Saturday morning cartoons and sitcoms and matinees, children grow up by themselves, without adult supervision or guidance, isolated in a convenient vacuum; but nature abhors a vacuum, and in the real world, kids grow up in families, nuclear and extended, and cobbled together.

They grow up in other people's houses and at school, in the mall, on the bus, at the park, on the sidewalk, in shelters, and on the streets. They grow up with Brian Williams and other newscasters, and the daily or on-line paper (or *The Enquirer*); they grow up overhearing our conversations about each other and the world. They grow up under billboards about alcohol, AIDS, and crack, and who to call if you find yourself pregnant. They grow up in a sexist, racist, greed-tilted world, with truth in advertising and government as much a fantasy as the Wicked-You-Know-What of the West.

Our children grow up in a world of vivisection, strip-mining and clear-cutting, a world of spectacular technological achievement and equally spectacular economic hypocrisy and squalor. They grow up in a world where injustice is denied or rationalized, a world that doubts the evidence of its senses and the importance of its longings.

Holding on, first to our fingers and later to our philosophies, our children are trying to keep their balance in this dizzying world. So are we. Wicca has helped us; and Wicca is the magical tool we can give to our children, just as the Goddess has given it to us.

We'll be talking about lots of things that indirectly relate to kids and families, same as we'd need to talk about gardens and vases if this were a book about bouquets. Now, the language available to us to talk about Wicca and its perspectives is still limited: patriarchal monotheism has dominated Western culture for a few years now, and dominates our language as well.

(This is why the word "witch" has such a bad reputation.) In this book, you'll see some effort to restore the balance, or at least remind us that it needs to be restored.

For instance, you'll see "s/he" instead of endless repetitions or alternations of "he and/or she." You'll also see "they" and "their" rather than "him and/or her" or "hers and/or his." You'll see "thealogy," too, reflecting the feminine nature of the generative principle; and sometimes "hera" as well as "hero," because we're all the champions of our lives' adventures. These aren't whimsical, or reverse sexisms, they're deliberate and precise usages. When this book first came out more than a decade ago, these were relatively unfamiliar usages; now they're more common. So is "God/dess," another word that's not merely convenient, but conveys a different meaning from "Goddess and/or God."

You'll notice as well that we use our Craft names throughout this book. Why? Are we hiding our identities because we're doing something bad and afraid of being found out? Nope. But people's civil names reveal what patriarchal society deems important about us—who our fathers are, mainly—while Craft names reflect what we (and sometimes our initiators) think is important about ourselves. Renaming ourselves in the Craft is an act of power, a power that some have always seen as threatening.

The use of our Craft names also expresses our solidarity with those of us who can't, even in the 21st century, come "out of the broom closet." (It's outrageous that any of us must keep our faith secret from our families, friends, and coworkers—and it's of no comfort at all that in the first few years of the 21st century, we're not the only religious group to feel the prejudice of ignorance and fear.)

By the way, in the first edition of this book, I did "reveal" my legal name, along with those of Canyondancer and our son, and in this edition, I don't. What's up with that? Happily, Craft names are well-enough understood, so the old point about not hiding anything doesn't need to be made quite so broadly or dramatically; 'dancer usually introduces himself by both names, so if you meet him, you'll hear it. The Explorer's legally an adult now, and his name is his, not mine, to share, so I'm following the rules of Craft etiquette by not "outing" him. (Or maybe, as he's not Wiccan now, I should say "inning" him!) And I've been to court to have my Craft name made legal (not instead of, but along with, my civil name; both are now on my driver's license and my passport). O'Gaea is the name I use in all priestessly and public situations, of which this is one.

You will read about covens in this book, too, because covens are important to children. A coven can be the multi-generational extended family kids would grow up in if we didn't have to move around to follow our jobs (or move into shelters when we lose our jobs). Coveners can be the aunts and uncles, brothers and sisters, or grandmas and grandpas who our kids don't get to spend time with. They are the other trusted adults from whom our children learn.

The coven is a healthy group to which our children can belong, and into which they can look forward to being initiated. Other writers remind us that, in the absence of wholesome social kinship groups into which they can grow, youngsters will meet that need as best they can, too often in gangs. The coven is the only place many of our kids can come to celebrate what's important to them, and to find help in working toward their goals.

Covens are also features of the landscape between the Worlds, where we hope our children will one day undertake their quests. Our coven/family—Campsight Coven—found camping a sort of between-the-Worlds experience, too.

One Ostara, the Explorer (who was not yet a teenager when I first wrote *Family Wicca*) and I had a long conversation about feeling like we were living in a magical story those three days at camp. The fact is, it got down to 20 degrees one night, but our effort was rewarded because that's how magical stories go: you brave the challenge to win riches you never imagined.

Not everyone sees it that way, though; some people hate to camp! But even if camping weren't our best idea of a good time, we'd give it a try now and then anyway, and I'll tell you why. Camping is as close as you can get to the rural roots of our religion, a chance to go back to the Mother for rebirth without any funeral expenses. Camping can bring our lore to life, and it's relevant to our present (and growing) concerns for the environment and to our hopes for a biospherically integrated future; most kids enjoy it, given a fair chance.

Still, camping isn't the only way to have the sort of experience from which Wicca draws so many rites, traditions, and images. If you really can't stand to set foot on the naked planet, you'll have to find or devise other ways of recreating our mythical ancestral environment and experience for yourself. Explore your family's personal or ethnic heritage and forge a link to earlier cultures with it. Bring out or find an antique, roast hot dogs (and marshmallows!) in front of your fireplace, light the room with candles; fill your kitchen with the magical aromas of traditional recipes; dress ethnically; learn the language your ancestors spoke—Gaelic? French? Anglo-Saxon? Slavic? You'll think of ways to effectively recreate your own tradition's old days—and you can always camp later if you change your mind!

A tremendous number of Wiccans today are urban Witches. We buy our herbs and incenses at the local co-op or from catalogues. Few of us make our own tools; fewer of us have even a clue how to do that (despite instructions in several books), and not all of us have the inclination or skills required. We're used to meeting indoors now, and we're not as comfortable in the extremes of weather our Anglo-Celtic ancestors endured routinely. That's okay.

What's not okay is that community is one of Wicca's foundations, and Nature is another, and a lot of us don't get much of either. Wicca is a religion of experience, yet many of us never get the chance to share the ancestral experiences that are the basis of our ritual traditions. Camping, although unfamiliar to many and horrifying to some, can be a solution to both of these problems—which is why the big gatherings are so popular.

Camping isn't mandatory, it's not usually an initiatory task, and it's not something you have to do to be a Witch. It just makes it, believe it or not, a little easier.

Now, 10 years after this book was first published, there are a couple of things I need to add to this introduction. One is that many covens are pretty ephemeral, forming and disbanding fairly quickly. The form remains valid, but the coven your children join—assuming they stay Wiccan and are coveners as adults—will probably be a different one than the one you belong to when your kids are little.

(The coven that Canyondancer and I founded in 1991 dissolved, amicably, on its 13th anniversary at Bride of 2004. In the Adventure Tradition we founded and developed, Hearth's Gate Coven now succeeds Campsight, and in the next few years we expect that more solitaries and covens will ask for recognition that they, too, practice Adventure Wicca. In the meantime, most of our former coveners are still in town, and still friends. But of course the changes in all our lives that inspired the coven's dissolution have forged new relationships among us.)

The other thing is about our—Wicca's—history. A few years ago, I was alerted by Pete "Pathfinder" Davis, founder of the Aquarian Tabernacle Church, to a book called *The Triumph of the Moon*, by Ronald Hutton (Oxford University Press, 1999). It's still not widely read in the United States, and is still fairly controversial when it is read. It's unjust to summarize it so briefly, but it basically demonstrates that what we thought was Wicca's history is actually our lore. No proto-Wicca survived the Inquisition. No secret midnight covens met deep in the woods, no Witches like us were burned at the stake; nowhere near 9 million people were killed.

It's not disrespectful or disastrous to accept this. Wicca doesn't have to be pre-Christian (pre-Christian Paganisms were state religions, about as different from Wicca as you can get) to be valid; Hutton himself calls

Gardner an avatar. What we now know to be our lore is rich and inspiring, and our true history is something of which we can be proud; we're still making it! As a community leader, a coven priestess, a Wiccan writer and a plain ol' practicing Witch, I feel an even greater responsibility to Wicca now than when I believed it was thousands of years old, and an even greater honor to be so close to the beginning of such a significant religious movement. Some Wiccans are distressed, but Canyondancer and I are not, and we don't think you need to be either.

In accordance with much that I've learned in the more than a decade that has passed since I originally wrote *Family Wicca*, I've changed bits of the book in this edition. Appendix C is now about "perfect love and perfect trust" instead of being a list of catalogue sources. Of course, I've past-tensed, and updated some of the stories about the Explorer, who is now in his mid 20s! Where my own perspective on certain aspects of the Craft has changed, I've added to and deleted some of what I first wrote.

But never fear: *Family Wicca* is still about modern Wiccan family life. Remember when it didn't even cross your mind that your grade-school teacher had an ordinary life outside the classroom? Well, people are so interested in Wicca's Sabbats and Esbats, in our ritual and magic, that even we sometimes forget that Witches live in the ordinary world, too. This book (still) remembers.

Chapter One

What Is a Modern Wiccan Family?

What is a modern Wiccan family? Well, we're Wiccan, and relatively modern (I'm revising this on a computer, at least, whereas the first edition was originally written longhand and revised on a typewriter), and our family now consists of me and my husband, our dog, three cats, and a wider group of about 20 people we love and trust. The Explorer's still part of the family, of course, but he doesn't live with us now, and as I've said, he's not Wiccan anymore.

When this book was first written, our family configuration included our young son, who now lives on the other side of town and doesn't circle with us any more. Our dear friend Faerie Moon, who was a charter member of our coven, divorced the Norseman, remarried a Pagan-friendly fellow, and now follows her own path of Shamanistic Witchcraft; she still circled with us once in a while until she moved to New Mexico. Canyondancer's brother Bilbo, once a member of Campsight, now lives on the other side of the country and doesn't circle with us anymore, either.

Merry meet! I'm O'Gaea—that's oh-gee-uh, as in, Oh, *gee*, uh…I don't know how to pronounce that! And I've already introduced Canyondancer.

We've moved since the first edition of *Family Wicca* was published, and we live at the new house—which is a traditionstead, rather than a covenstead—with our dog, Barleycorn, and the current trio of cats: Hal, Milo, and Bette Noire. We still live in Tucson, Arizona, though, and Tucson's still a pretty good place to be a Witch.

We've been Wiccan for two decades now—or all our lives, depending on how you look at it. I was still a kid when my mom, who wasn't Wiccan (but came from a pretty witchy family), told me that "Christmas came from Solstice." "Solstice" is what I've been celebrating ever since. Canyondancer's story is similar. When the Explorer was born, close to 27 years ago, we decided to stop calling it "Christmas"—to stop describing the world in Christian terms.

My mom's family, Welsh and Scottish, has always been visionary and psychic. My dad's side, English and Irish, taught me about herbs. Canyondancer's mom and her people, Irish and Scottish, had the Sight. None of them called themselves Witches—they were everything from Presbyterian to freethinkers, Episcopal to agnostic—but they seemed witchy enough to us!

Canyondancer and I were married more than 30 years ago in a Unitarian church, and in Tucson we were active in the Unitarian-Universalist church for about 10 years before we needed something more. When we left the church, looking for something more participatory and compelling, more immediate and yet more mythical, Faerie Moon gave me a copy of *Drawing Down the Moon*.

I read it and then *The Spiral Dance* in quick succession, and we never looked back. Canyondancer and I initiated each other to First Degree a couple of years later, at midnight one Samhain (and the candles sputtered and flared at all the right moments). I took my Third Degree from two eclectic priestess here just before the 1990s Summer Solstice; Canyondancer took his a few months later. With Faerie Moon and the Explorer, we declared Campsight Circle a full-fledged coven at Bride of 1991.

Mind, we'd been keeping Sabbats and Moons for some time. Canyondancer and I called ourselves solitaries who happened to be married and working together. The Explorer worked with us now and again, and participated in all our Sabbats and Esbats. Faerie Moon and her then-husband, the Norseman, were another solitary Witch and her husband who joined us for many Suns and Moons. When asked if we were a coven, we said for many years that we weren't.

It wasn't only the number of years we'd been Witches together that led us to formalize Campsight, though. It was also the fact that all of us were able to be straightforward about our faith, and we felt that gave us an obligation to stand up, even stand *out*, for our brothers and sisters in the Craft who couldn't do the same. Faerie Moon, 'dancer, and I had talked to people about Wicca for years, answering questions and correcting misunderstandings. We wrote a number of flyers to hand out when we started conversations we couldn't quite finish on the bus or with clients and patients. We'd been doing that, and the odd radio shows, television appearances, lectures, and workshops, for a long time.

Our decision to make Campsight an official coven, then, was in some way *political*. Spiritually, we were and are dedicated to the God/dess, and to Wicca's model of the world as a friendly, family- and growth-oriented place. We'd earned the right to call ourselves a coven by our religious study and dedication; and we also felt entitled to whatever "socio-political" security and authority a coven offers. Campsight grew relatively old before it disbanded at Bride in 2004—but the God/dess knew us before we encovened, and still knows us now that Campsight is history.

We raised the Explorer to the Craft, and he was a member of our coven as naturally as he was a member of our family. At his first dedication, near his seventh birthday, he was able to commit to the Goddess' service in terms of respecting life and helping to take care of the environment. Later, he could cast a Circle with us, and he had a coming-of-age rite when he entered his teens.

The older he got, and the more concerned with the affairs of the world-that-is-wider-than-our-neighborhood, the more he learned to appreciate Wicca. There were occasional complaints about turning off the television or putting down what he was reading when it was time for a Circle, but when the ritual began, his attention was better focused each time.

Is that your child? Wicca's tenets made sense to him and he found encouragement in Witchcraft's morality. Now, the same as then, it can be tough to make sense of the world, but Wicca's teachings are a helpful framework for understanding. Witchcraft's wide perspective, both global and historical, is a context for patterns of events. Wicca's confidence in the loving nature of life and its emphasis on family guarantees that all of us can get a hug when we need one.

Other Witches we know count as family good friends as well as blood relations. Some of our friends have babies, some are single parents, some have grown children, and some have no children; some are straight, some are gay. So what's a family? A family is any group of people who know each other well and love each other anyway! Family are those people who nurture us and affirm us, who delight in and contribute to our growth, and grow right along with us.

The family is humanity's natural social unit, and arguably the model for covens, which are representations of the cosmos. Starhawk says that in Wicca's context we can call it "love" that holds atoms together in the forms we inhabit and take for granted. Similarly, life, the universe, and everything is one big family, and all of us are favored children.

In a more prosaic sense, are we a traditional family? Not statistically. We had 1.0 children, not 2.8. For years we had only one car and one income; 'dancer tended the home fires while I worked in a law office. Househusbandry, we are pleasantly surprised to see, is becoming more common, even though it's because more men than women are being laid off during the tough economic times we're going through in the early 2000s.

A few years ago, it was 'dancer and I who moved out when the Explorer grew up! For a few years we had a VW camper in addition to the car we drive most of the time, though as I revise these pages, we've just gotten a pop-up camp trailer to replace the VW. Since my parents died, I've retired to write and present workshops; 'dancer, bless him, is still a house-husband. We weren't (and still aren't) socio-culturally traditional—are you?

When Canyondancer and I announced our engagement, another old and dear friend, a "sister with different parents" who is now a Presbyterian minister, made us a plaque that said,

> *True love is not looking at each other,*
> *it's gazing outward in the same direction.*

This made sense to us, and still does, and it's become a part of our understanding of family.

Canyondancer and I made certain choices—that one of us would stay home with our child, for instance, even though it reduced our income—in favor of the family life we wanted. We're aware that many things would have been different if we hadn't had a child, and that many things could have been different if we'd raised him differently. We made all our choices with our eyes open, willing to accept the consequences even if we couldn't anticipate all of them.

And now, "consequences," with its negative connotations, doesn't seem like the right word to use. All we gave up were a few *things*, and we didn't miss any of them. What we had—still have—instead is more precious than the richest collection of possessions: unconditional love and peace, and in that, the only real security there is.

(Let me add some clarification here about "unconditional love." At the 2003 Pagan Unity Festival, I got a copy of Grey Cat's wonderful book, *Deepening Witchcraft*, and read what she had to say on pages 337–338: "Unconditional love is a concept I am most uncomfortable with. It seems to me that if another entity loves me regardless of what I do, that's more undiscerning than unconditional.... Let's ask of the God/desses and perhaps of a few people close to us for free and unconstrained love, but not undeserved and indiscriminate love. This is a love which can endure when we screw up, but notices when that happens and supports our efforts to do better." Well, *yes*. But that's what I understand "unconditional love" to mean—love that notices our mistakes without withdrawing, love that not only supports but expects us to work at doing better. Love that doesn't expect growth is not, in my opinion, worth the effort of giving or accepting.)

Our family is united by many values and attitudes, all of them directly or indirectly Wiccan. As the Explorer's grown up, our relationship with him has changed. Faerie Moon's resignation from the coven changed things, too, as did her move to New Mexico. Campsight's membership changed many times over the years, and so have our personal circumstances. Change is what we worship, though, for change makes growth possible, and growth is what life—and families—are all about.

Your family is united by shared values and attitudes, too, and your family is growing and changing, as all families do. All of us can find power in change, and the power to shape those changes to our will. That's the very heart of family life—and of Witchcraft. *As you will, so mote it be.* Families, yours and mine, are what we make of them, you and me.

Our life as a family of Witches is full and satisfying. Wicca permeates our lives, enriches our lives, guides our lives. In this book, we'll share some of our traditions, rituals, and songs; some of the problems we've encountered, and our best solutions for them; and some of our thoughts about life, the universe, and everything.

And oh, yes—10 years on, you may wonder, how the Explorer is doing? Well, later in this book, I state that not all of our children are going to be Wiccan when they grow up, and I've emphasized that "that has to be okay." Right here and now I can tell you that it *is* okay.

The Explorer no longer considers himself Wiccan—he doesn't follow any religion, in fact. But he's still respectful of the environment, and of everyone's right to follow their own bliss. He doesn't circle with us now, but he still comes to video some of our Sabbats for us. He's a man now, and a good man; we're proud of him. Even though he doesn't see them in religious terms anymore, he still follows the precepts he learned as a Wiccan kid.

At left, a 6-year-old Explorer peers out from Tom Sawyer's cave at Disneyland; at right, a 24-year-old Explorer pauses for a moment in his parents' library.

The Explorer is our biological son, but not every family that includes children is made up, or entirely made up, of children born to the parents who raise them. I have relatives and friends who were adopted in their infancy, and because my own parents held ugly prejudices against adoptees, I grew up believing it was "best" if the fact and process of adoption should not be brought up. The first edition of *The Family Wicca Book* didn't discuss adoption, but it's a topic I now believe needs attention.

Only in the last few years have "open adoptions," in which the birthmother and the adopting parents meet, and the birthmother has contact with the children she bears for the adopting family, gained any acceptance. It may be, too, that a few years ago it would have been difficult for openly Pagan couples to adopt, but Neo-Pagan faiths are better accepted now, and our opportunities are widening. So, too, is our understanding of the "other side" of adoption—the birthmother's experience and decision to relinquish her child to someone else's care. I'm sorry that I didn't think years ago to talk about all this in *Family Wicca*, but glad I have the idea and opportunity to do so in the second edition!

The following discussion and rituals, though they're in a segment about adoption, are not useful only to people involved in adoptions. Children who will stay with and be raised by their birthparents should also be blessed and welcomed; parents who are raising their biological children have as much need to make a fuss and swear allegiance to the baby (and the adult he or she will become) as any adopting families do. So at the same time you allow what you read next to deepen your understanding of the adoption experience, understand it as something you can use if your are a soon-to-be parent, too!

Adoption

When a friend brought bits of her manuscript to our writing group, I was horrified to see that her research shows that many feminist authors decry adoption, arguing that abortion is the only politically correct alternative to "keeping the baby." Golly! Yes, alright, adoption is touted by right-wing fundamentalists, and it can be unnerving to find oneself in their camp, but rejecting adoption because you aren't comfortable with who else supports it *is* rather the ultimate "throwing the baby out with the bathwater."

Studies indicate that both birthmothers and adoptees feel the process as a wound, one that is difficult to heal. Adopted friends say that even as adults, and even knowing the circumstances their birthmothers were in, they can't help wondering why they were rejected. My author-friend, a birthmother herself, can still weep with the grief (along with some occasional twinges of guilt) she feels for relinquishing her children, even though she bore them specifically for the family who lovingly received them, and even though she still has a relationship with them.

My adopted friend's case was closed: she'll never know her birthmother, and she points out that one problem with that is that she doesn't know her medical history, or whether she has siblings. My friend the birthmother, for whom the adoptions are open, reports that one of the children she bore seems to be grappling with feelings of rejection even though both of his mothers are caring and attentive. So, whether an adoption is closed and shrouded with shame or open and undertaken as a gift, there's a great deal of pain involved. Does this mean we should reject adoption as an alternative to abortion or childlessness?

Well, no.

Avoiding pain isn't life's purpose. Of course, suffering isn't life's purpose, either. It seems to me—and admittedly, I speak without any personal experience of adoption—that one issue here is religious, and that's how we look at emotional pain; and another is social, and that's how we look at reproduction. Although Canyondancer and I both advise parents to be aware of their sociopolitical positions and how those affect their behavior, this book doesn't need to emphasize politics...so let's take a look at the big facet of the religious issue—how we look at emotional pain.

Pain is energy. Wiccans, being Witches, work with energy. If we find energy unconstructive in one form, we can "spin" it until it takes a form with which we can work. To work with any energy, we have to identify and acknowledge it, and the same goes for pain. You know, if a person, say, breaks her leg, she looks at the wound, says, "Oh, sugar! My leg's broken! Get me to the emergency room!" But if we are wounded emotionally, we're much more likely to say, "Oh, er, um, no, really, I'm okay." Many of us are convinced that acknowledging emotional pain is a sign of weakness, and that identifying it is either impossible or going to make it worse. My opinion is that this is utter nonsense.

If something hurts, see what it is, and deal with it. Sure, sometimes you have to live with certain kinds of pain—but let's look at why that is. It's because the energy it takes to ease the pain is more than it takes to endure it. That's why some people decide against chemotherapy, for instance, or, less alarmingly, why some people wait for a good night's sleep to ease muscle pain rather than rushing off to take a pill at the first twinge. As I type these words, my psoriasis is acting up and my hand itches fearfully. I could go and smear the prescription goo on the flare-ups and cover them with plastic wrap and tape to keep it in place, but the time and attention that would take would derail my train of thought, and I'd have to spend a lot longer working on this segment. So instead, I'm using the throbbing itch as a kind of a beat to work to, like music for aerobics. I can do this because I know that my psoriasis is not life-threatening, and that it will progress in a couple of days to a stage that doesn't itch—and I know that when I'm done at the keyboard, if I want to, I can go get the medicine.

Now, getting back to adoption. My adopted friend has actually seen the records of her relinquishment, and knows that although her birthmother was not blameless in conceiving a child "on the wrong side of the sheets," as they used to say, her birthmother was pretty unselfish in giving the baby up for adoption. With her adoptive parents, my friend had opportunities she would not likely have enjoyed had her birthmother kept her. There would have been a divorce, and probably there would have been either poverty or relinquishment at a later date, or both; and there might have been a good deal of resentment, too. Knowing that giving her up was her birthmother's last, best gift to her, makes it, sometimes, a little easier to accept. There are still fantasies about the fairy-tale life she might have had with her birthparents, but there's always the hard-landing reality that her mother's husband would not have loved her as his own, because she wasn't: her birthmother had conceived her on "the wrong side of the sheets." Her adoptive parents literally chose her from among several babies lined up in their basinets; in their lives, she was no mistake.

My friend who has borne children for another family did so deliberately—she was not rescued from an accidental pregnancy by their willingness to adopt. I take her at her word that she feels guilty about "giving up" those children, but I will admit to having some trouble understanding that feeling. These children came from her body, but they were always intended for the arms of their adoptive parents. Yes, my friend bonded with her infants before they went home, at 3-days-old, with their new parents, and, of course, her body needed to grieve their loss. I know that my bewilderment at her feelings of having done something wrong is a function of my inexperience with the situation, and not a fault in her emotional circuits. I just wish there was something I could do or say to help her, and my adopted friend, spin that energy so that it continues to nourish their growth.

What the birthmother in my writing group says is that not many books, when they address the subject of adoption at all, consider it in a positive light. As I've said, I don't "get that." In my son's baby book, we pasted a quote from Alistair Clarke (as he wrote in *One Man's America*): "In the best of times our days are numbered anyway. And so it would be a crime against nature for any generation to take the world crisis so solemnly that it put off enjoying those things for which we were presumably designed in the first place...the opportunity to do good work, to fall in love, to enjoy friends, to hit a ball and to bounce a baby."

I think it applies just as well to adoption. When we make babies, we are making a gift, to the child, to ourselves, and to whomever's lives he or she touches, to the whole world, to life itself, and to the God/dess. This is a blessing, this is glorious. And you know, whether we send our babies off to other families when they're 3 days old, or off to college or their own apartment or the armed forces when they're age 18, at some point we do have to send them off. What's important is not whether this is painful, but that we send them with our blessings, and that they know it.

Granted, a three-day-old child can't understand the withdrawal of the birthmother's breast as a bon voyage—not immediately, anyway. Granted, it's a wound—but wounds can be recovered from, and not all scars are debilitating or disfiguring. Nobody has to be "poor baby" just because s/he was adopted.

A few years ago, I found a vigorous discussion on an e-mail forum about parental responsibilities. One group of posters insisted that a parent's job is to keep young children from suffering of any kind; the rest of us were just as sure that no, a parent's job is to help a child learn how to cope with pain of various sorts. Raise your hand if you've been able to keep yourself from suffering of any kind. And then explain how, because if you can't keep pain out of your own life, you expect to "protect" your children from it.

Let's say your toddler's toddling his merry way down the front walk and you see him about to step in front of an oncoming car. You rush down there, screaming (scaring the child silly), and then reach forth rather violently to keep him from getting run over. Okay. You've saved him from being hit by the car. In the process of grabbing him to safety, you may have bruised his arms or ribs. Your emotional intensity, your loud shouting, and your physical abruptness have frightened and bodily hurt him. Should you not have intervened?

Adoption is a much less violent removal of some children from harm's way, and a fairly nonviolent way to give them the blessings of a loving family and various material advantages that a birthparent may not be able to provide. Some feminists worry that advocating adoption will threaten the already tenuous legal status of abortion, and maybe that's a fair concern. Abortion is and should always be a legal alternative to a full-term pregnancy—but I am pro-choice, and that means as many choices as possible, and that means including adoption. Neither I nor Wicca will presume to tell a woman whether she should rejoice in or reject being pregnant. But I will say that I expect both my religion and my government to give every woman as wide a range of choices as Nature allows.

But society still tends to look at adoption as something shameful, from both sides. We, too, often assume that a woman relinquishing her child for adoption is immoral, has gotten "knocked up" accidentally and doesn't want the baby, or is the victim of rape or incest and can't stand to look at the spawn. And we, too, often see adoptive couples as reproductively inadequate, barren or impotent, or afflicted with some disease or genetic condition they wouldn't dare pass on. Even with so much pro-life posturing and family-values fuss going on, we put a lot of conditions on our appreciation of pregnancy and birth and parenting.

What if we try thinking of it as wonderful? As something "full of wonder," or "awesome." What if we try thinking of it as a precious and sacred part of the process of life and growth and death and rebirth? What if we think of conception and pregnancy and birth and adoption as holy and what if we think of our responses to these events as rituals, as offerings to deity? How would that change the way we see adoption?

It might inspire us to show respect toward birthmothers for their courage in staying pregnant and giving birth to a child they may never know, even though they may be harassed in many ways for their decisions. It might inspire us to see giving birth as taking a woman beyond her personal identity to a universal, symbolic womanness or goddesshood. It might allow us to see adoptive parents as receiving red, squalling, wiggling bundles of living divinity, as priest/esses to the god/dess in their arms.

Canyondancer and I have long taught an attitude we call regency parenting (see *Raising Witches*, New Page Books, 2002), and this regency we all undertake for our children is, perhaps, a little more obvious when parents are accepting it for a child of someone else's body. Perhaps understanding adoption as a sacred act can help us understand life's interconnectedness a little better, and a little more personally.

It seems to me that in addition to the process of adopting a child (including the birthmother's experience of conception, gestation, birth, and relinquishment, being one of those mundane sequences that is a de facto ritual), there are at least three or four specific rituals that should bless particular aspects of adoption. Of course, there could be many, beginning with conception, and marking the stages of pregnancy; every meeting of birthmother with adoptive parents could include a ritual. These are details that the participants in these events need to notice and arrange for themselves. We'll just suggest a few ideas to get people started looking at these things in a more sensible way than society currently sees them.

Blessing the Conception of an Adopted Child

This ritual can be done as soon as the birthmother knows she's pregnant with a child she's carrying for someone else, or as soon as adoptive parents know that someone is carrying the child they will raise. If the adoptive parents never meet their baby's birthmother, they can do this ritual themselves, and no matter how old the "baby" is. This ritual blesses an act, decision, and/or condition, not a moment.

In addition to your usual Altar gear (minimal or full), you'll need a baby bottle (with nipple), talcum powder or cornstarch, soft music, pleasant incense and/or oil, some wine or hot tea (this will be the rite's "ale"— whether cakes are included is up to you), a pencil or cuticle stick, an 8-inch length of white ribbon, and some clay (whether you use the kind that needs to be fired in a kiln, or the kind you can bake in your oven is up to you. You will need enough to make a ball about the size of your palm.

Cast a Circle in a place that is private, calm, and seems to you conducive of sacred conception. Play the soft music; make sure you won't be bothered by the harsh sounds of tapes ending or CDs changing, or interrupted by an anomalous song. Fill the baby bottle with water. Set it in the West—on the Altar or at the Quarter, as you prefer. Set the talcum powder or cornstarch at East.

When you cast the Circle with Fire, make it the Fire of holy passion for life. When you cleanse the Circle with Salt and Water, make it the salty water of the womb. When you charge the Circle with Air, make it the air that carries scents, ideas, and understanding. For this you can use either the talcum powder, to remind you of babies, or a romantic incense, to remind you of making the love that babies come from.

When you call the Quarters, look for their contributions to care and commitment, patience, unconditional love, common sense, openness, and other such qualities that are helpful both in conceiving and raising children. When you invoke the Gods, invoke Them as lovers, Her as Mother, and Him as brother/child.

If you are a woman conducting this ritual alone, use the oil to anoint yourself or the incense to smudge yourself in a version of the five-fold kiss. (No, you don't have to be a contortionist. You might like to use a mirror, though. You don't have to be skyclad, but that's appropriate; there does need to be some respectful, admiring, loving touching going on, though.) If you are a committed couple, go as far as you like in the love-making process, but remember that it's the conception of a child, and a specific child, even if s/he's still unmet, that this rite honors.

When your body and mood are focused on conceiving this child, put all hands on the mother's (birth or adoptive) womb, and say these or your own similar words:

Blesséd be this gathering of energy within.

Blesséd be the heart(s) and mind(s) that let new life begin.

Blesséd be this planting of the precious sacred seed.

Blesséd be the knowing and the meeting of the need.

Blessed be this conception and the love that makes us kin.

(If this ritual is being performed by and for a receiving mother who has no womb, her own and any other hands participating should be placed over her heart; of course, that's an option in any case.)

Now consecrate and share the wine or tea. As you sip, the mother should make first a ball and then a disc with the clay. Everyone present should press a fingertip into it. You might use the tip of your "power finger" (pointer finger of your dominant hand), or the tip of a pinky, which is more like a baby's finger. You might prefer to make an impression of your wedding ring. If you'd rather seal a kiss onto this talisman, put the kiss on the tip of your finger first; lips don't make very attractive (or iconic) impressions in clay. On the other side of the disc, you may wish to commemorate the ritual with an inscription, but you don't have to. Use the pencil or cuticle stick to poke a hole through the disk; when it's fired or dry, you'll put the ribbon through the hole so you can hang the disk.

Before you close the Circle, bless the ribbon, which is not only the hanger for the disc, but also represents the umbilical cord, the "silver cord" that binds our ethereal bodies to our physical bodies, and the lines of the Web of Wyrd. You can use your own rite of consecration, or something like this:

Little ribbon, be the cord

along which all our love is poured.

Be rays that find and ties that bind:

> *connect us, heart and soul and mind.*
> *We're always bound but ever free,*
> *As [I/we] will, so mote it be.*

Now, finish the tea, close the Circle, and remember this rite whenever you need some patience or other parental strength.

Birth Blessings for a Child Who Will Be Adopted

Here are a couple of blessings for a child who will be adopted. Either or both may be given at any time within a day or so of the birth.

For the woman bearing the child, there may not be time or energy available during the birth; the woman adopting may not know exactly when the process of birth begins. If she knows the birthmother, she may get a call when contractions starts or the water breaks, and that would be an ideal time for both mothers to bless the coming baby. However, birth blessings will be effective if given anytime in the first 48 hours of the child's life, and may be given even later, if "later" is when the receiving mother gets news of the birth. Fathers, other family members, and close friends may, of course, participate!

Furthermore, no harm at all will come from giving a blessing more than once. It's not uncommon for the birth of a baby, and the very sight of a newborn, to inspire awe and reverence, and a sense of remarkably combined delicacy and strength, immediacy and timelessness. Whatever their effects may be when repeated at 3 a.m. for several days, the first scents and sounds a new baby makes quite often enhance this sense of wonder. The thought of this "fragile little beast" being sent into the unknown—even a reasonably well-known unknown—can inspire repeated blessings, which we should think of as measures of care rather than assessments of danger.

Burrow Blessing

Burrow, burrow into life

Come out, come out, emerge and thrive!

Go from womb to arms, to arms

Receive the love; reject alarm

Our hearts protect you from all harm.

Burrow, burrow from the womb

Safe in our love, come out and bloom!

Blesséd Baby

Blesséd baby, we await

your birth, and, baby, bless your fate.

Who you will be we cannot say,

But we'll all love you anyway.

Three mothers' love looks out for you:

one gives you birth,

to one you go forth

and with you always is Mother Earth.

Baby, as you come our way,

this we call a blesséd day!

Whenever a baby is taken from the mother who has given it birth, no matter what her mind knows of the matter, her body insists on grieving the loss. There is nothing we can or should do to prevent a mother from going through this process—it is natural and necessary. It is appropriate, though, to help the mother who is sending her child to adoptive parents feel that both the baby's and her own life will go on, and to good purpose.

This rite combines some ways of helping a birthmother find this feeling. It offers her some tangible mementos that are given specific meanings in an order and arrangement that refocus her on the cycle of life, and it offers comforting sounds, sights, scents, and touches. It allows the mother to experience the same unconditional love she has for her infant, and must trust that her infant will have from the adopting family. It reinforces her sense of belonging, recharges her spirit, and allows her to identify with her baby by suggesting that she, too, is beginning a new [phase of her] life.

A Rite to Bless the Birthmother

You will need three charms for this rite, and a necklace, bracelet, or pin on which the birthmother can wear them; you may make them yourself or buy them at a store. One will represent the baby, one the adoptive family, and one the birthmother herself. Consecrate the charms before you perform this rite. Ideally, a member of the birthmother's family will consecrate the charm representing the adoptive family, the birthmother will consecrate the charm that represents the baby, and those friends and family closest to the birthmother will consecrate the charm that represents her. (If the relationship between the birthmother and the adoptive family makes it appropriate, a member of that family might participate in the consecration of the charm that represents the birthmother.) In any case, the consecration of all the charms should be done by people who genuinely care for the well-being of the people the charms represent.

Depending on what you have chosen to hold the charms, you may need a pair of pliers, and, if the room is cozily dim, you may also need a small flashlight to use while attaching the charms to whatever chain, pin, or ribbon will hold them.

This rite is best done with at least five people (in addition to the birthmother, who takes a very receptive role). More people will enhance the rite; but if fewer are available, be creative. Whatever modifications are made should retain the tender, care-taking feel of this rite.

Define the Circle with potpourri or ribbons perfumed in the birthmother's favorite scent. If pictures of birthmother and baby are available, frame one nicely at North and set a tea light beside it. Mark the Quarters "romantically," with white or ivory pillar candles that are pleasantly scented, and with "earth toned" symbols. Set an Altar in the North East (leaving room for a Door), and make a comfortable place for the birthmother in the center.

Have on hand for Cakes and Ale some chamomile tea and some delicious little tea cakes that the birthmother favors. Make more herb tea available than sweets: a sugar rush can feel good, but it's not quite consistent with the feeling this rite aims to produce (also be prepared to cut a Door as many times as the birthmother needs to go out and urinate).

At each Quarter, position a loving friend. East will hold the charm representing the baby, South will hold the charm representing the adoptive family, West will hold the charm representing the birthmother, and North will hold the necklace, bracelet, or pin that will hold all three charms. A fourth individual will function as the priest/ess; this person's relationship to the birthmother is more important than his/her gender.

Agree ahead of time on some simple tune—perhaps a lullaby or something else that the birthmother likes—which can be hummed slowly through most of the ritual, and which is easy to hum in harmony.

The birthmother might like to take a relaxing bath and will certainly want to dress comfortably before this rite begins. Before she enters the Circle, she should see and hear the Circle being cast, cleansed, and charged. Before the Quarters are called, she should enter (or be led in by the priest/ess) and get comfy. (She'll let you know whether she wants blankets and pillows arranged on the floor, or a chair and footstool, or something else/more.)

When the birthmother is ensconced, the priest/ess calls the Quarters, with these words or others written especially for the occasion.

Hail, Old Ones of the East, Guardians of Air. As you shelter and cherish all that is new, shelter and cherish [*birthmother's name*] as a new day dawns for her. Show her the beauty of her choice, and give her the gift of clear memories.

East, humming the agreed-upon tune softly, comes forward and gives the birthmother the baby charm. Still humming, East returns to the Quarter—and will continue to hum softly.

The priest/ess then calls South:

Hail, Old Ones of the South, Guardians of Fire. As you enflame [*birthmother's name*] heart with courage, let her feel us standing beside her. Show her the bravery of her choice, and give her the gift of confidence.

South, joining East in humming, comes forward and gives the birthmother the adopting family charm. Still humming, South returns to the Quarter—and like East, continues humming.

Now the priest/ess calls West:

Hail, Old Ones of the West, Guardians of Water. As you swell [*birthmother's name*] love for [*baby's name*], let her feel our love for her. Show her how to receive our care and blessing, and give her the gift of friendship.

West, starting to hum with East and South, steps into the center to give the birthmother the charm that represents her. West keeps humming, perhaps adding harmony, and returns to the Quarter.

Finally, the priest/ess calls North:

Hail, Old Ones of the North, Guardians of Earth. As you restore [*birthmother's name*] vitality, let her feel that we are among her resources. Show her how to find her inner strength, and give her the gift of continuity.

Now North begins to hum and comes to give the birthmother the necklace or other item that will connect the charms. At this point, the rest of the Quarters come to the center so that they and the priest/ess surround the birthmother fairly closely. If she is on the floor, they will want to kneel or sit around her, not crowding her, but within arm's reach. They are still humming.

The priest/ess [still standing] now calls upon Spirit:

From the center of our Circle, from the center of our beings, we call upon Spirit, the spirit of the Spiral Dance of Life. As you fill us all, assure us that love knows no limits in time or space. Assure us that true family cannot be sundered by months or miles. Give us the gift of knowing life's harmony.

As the priest/ess speaks, the Quarters are helping the birthmother attach the charms to the chain, pin, or ribbon. Humming continues until the charms are attached and the necklace or bracelet has been put on the birthmother, or the pin affixed to her clothing. At this point, if the birthmother is comfortable standing up, she rises and joins the others, entwining with their arms and swaying slightly to the rhythm of the tune. If she would rather stay seated, the others move a little closer to her so they can all touch and hum together.

If there are words to the tune (original or filked), start singing them now. Otherwise, continue humming, a little louder and with as much harmony as the group can manage. The priest/ess will know when the energy is at its peak, and direct the others to hold the birthmother's hands to give her this very mellow energy. One by one, first the birthmother, then the priest/ess, then North, West, South, and East stop humming and the room becomes silent.

If the birthmother is comfortable with the idea, excess energy can be grounded by people stroking her aura, sweeping their hands from the top of her head to the ground. The priest/ess should use his/her judgement in this; if the birthmother needs physical stroking or a hug, she should have it!

When everyone is calm again, the priest/ess acknowledges Spirit and the Quarters:

> *In harmony are we restored,*
> *our hearts and minds in new accord.*
> *By motherhood* [birthmother's name] *blessed**
> *She raised her child to* [*his or her*] *life's quest.*
> *Directions guide, Spirit abide,*
> *yet go as ye will: we're sanctified.*
> *We do ordain that love remain,*
> *as in thanks ebbs our Circle's tide.*

* If her name doesn't fit the meter, try adding an "our" before it, or say "our friend is."

This rite is not ended with conventional formal thanks or Quarter releases because you've established a very gentle atmosphere here, one of trust and safety and rest. To send the Quarters physically back to their stations on the circumference of the Circle would be disruptive. The rhyming thanks and release is more in keeping with the serenity this rite creates. If you feel the need to dismiss them more ceremonially, do so from the center and as softly as possible.

Rather than extinguishing the Quarter candles, if they have been on the floor around the Circle, move them now to furniture close to their appropriate directions, and let them burn a little longer. (Of course, you mustn't leave them burning unattended, but it might be pleasant to sit a little longer, together, in candlelight before turning the glaring electrics back on.) Save them so that when the birthmother wishes to reexperience the "vibe" of this rite, she can relight them (or replenish them with tea lights) and hum to herself.

The same group of friends who officiated at this blessing may wish to occasionally present the birthmother with an additional (consecrated) charm to mark milestones in the child's life, if the birthmother shares news of them.

The formalities of adoption vary from state to state. However, in every case there will be some signing of papers, and that's always going to be a momentous occasion. It may not be possible to sign the necessary papers in a formally cast Circle, but it is possible for the birthmother, and others who will be present, to ground and center before going to the place where the papers are to be signed. The birthmother will undoubtedly be given copies of these papers for her own records and, once home, can certainly consecrate those, and through them, the process and act of transferring legal parenthood.

The same goes for the members of the adopting family. Legal responsibility for a child is important to establish, of course, and formalizing it is an important occasion. However, parenthood is more than legal responsibility. It's a sacred trust, and the legal formalities don't formalize that aspect of the arrangement. It's up to the adopting parents to do that on their own.

Can the giving birthmother and the receiving family be at cross-purposes if they both consecrate their adoption papers? Well, of course they can—but we don't recommend doing any religious rites or magic motivated by anger or a desire for revenge, or to get out of an agreement. We hope for the sake of the child (and everyone else) that every adoption arrangement goes smoothly, and that the birthmother and the adopting family will maintain a relationship. While we understand that children need consistency in their upbringing, and know that playing children for pawns is always "a bad thing," we also believe that no child can have too many people interested in its welfare and care, and who want to be supportive.

So when we suggest that both the birthmother and the adopting family consecrate the baby's new circumstances, with the adoption papers as the focus of the rite, we intend for all parties to be committing themselves to the service of the child's best interests, not their own at the child's expense. (And we'd like to add that this should be the case for parents who are raising their biological children, too. More of our specific ideas about parenting are explored in *Raising Witches*.)

Parenting Oath and Consecration of Adoption Papers

Do this as part of a formally cast Circle. You can choose a specially significant time, or do it in one of your regular Esbats. Whenever in the rite you would normally perform magic is the right time to do this. You will need a certified copy of the adoption document (not your *only* certified copy, but not just a photocopy of a certified copy, either), some Dragon's Blood or other magical ink, a quill, and a candle in a color you find suitable for Oath-making.

If the adoption document is one or two pages long, you will write your Oath on the first page. If it is longer than two pages, you have the option of writing your Oath on the second page. If you make such a choice, write your reasons for it in your Book of Shadows.

In the Circle (but before you write your Oath), cleanse the document with all the elements and cleanse yourself that you may be of pure heart and mind when you make this Oath. You may write it out ahead of time on a separate piece of paper and copy if from that paper onto the adoption document. Do not write on the adoption document ahead of time. (The magical reason for this is that the Oath will carry more weight if the first time you write it is the only time. The practical reason is that in candlelight you won't be able to see anything you've penciled in anyway. You do not want to distract this spell with a flashlight, which in this case would be an intrusion of the rational world into what should be an activity of the heart and soul.)

Another choice you have is whether to position the adoption document with the writing right side up or upside down. Write your reasons for this choice, too, in your Book of Shadows. (Indeed, we suggest that you devote one page in your Book of Shadows to every adoption ritual you do, leaving room to record your thoughts and feelings at least once a year for at least five years. No matter your role in the child's life, participation in parenting constitutes the longest spell you will ever cast!)

Leave space on your Altar, or have another hard surface available, to put the adoption document to write on it. When you are ready, between the lines of the adoption document (or on top of them if it's happens to be single spaced), write the following Oath. Of course, you may modify this as you see fit; and of course we recommend that modifications be only to make the Oath more personal, and not less difficult or binding.

Adoption / Parent's Oath

I/we [your name(s)] *vow*
that I/we shall ever hold holy
and respect and cherish this charge:
to defend [child's name] *title to* [his/her] *life,*
to prepare [him/her] *to claim* [his/her] *own authority,*
and to accord [him/her] *Goddess-speed on* [his/her] *quest*
and hinder [him/her] *not in undertaking it.*
I/we will never exploit
nor ever deny this gift of life and love.
I/we do vow this in the sight and names
of the Gods and the Mighty Ones
and pledge it on my/our own life/lives.

When you have written this Oath on the adoption document, sign it with both your civil name(s) and your magical name(s). Then, light your

"Oath-colored" candle and as you read the Oath aloud, drip some of its wax on your civil signature. If you are right-handed, press your right thumb into the wax; if you're left-handed, press your left thumb into it, to seal your signature. Next, read the Oath aloud again, and this time drip Oath-candle wax on your magical signature and press your other thumb into it to seal it.

You have made and sealed the Oath both mundanely and magically, in your left brain and in your right, in this world and all the worlds. Now it's time to consecrate the signed, sealed document, and with it, the Oath itself. If you have a consecration rite in your Book of Shadows, use it. If your rite requires a name for the object to be consecrated, call this your Parent's Oath, for though it is made on an adoption document, you are a parent, and you have made a parent's oath. (It would not be the least bit inappropriate for adopting or biological parents to make this same oath on a certified copy of their child's birth certificate. Neither would it be inappropriate for any parents to renew the vow on the child's every birthday!)

If you need a Consecration, here's one you can use or modify. If more than one person is making this Oath, decide ahead of time whether both or all of you will hold the document together, take turns, or designate one of you to carry it. Regardless of how the document itself is handled, everyone making the Oath should walk around the Circle, approach the Altar, and speak the words.

In the center of your Circle, hold the document "above" for the space of three heartbeats. Then touch it to the ground ("below") for the space of another three heartbeats. Say: "I/we conjure this Oath and consecrate it to the sacred work of parenting, and affirm that I/we shall use it for nothing malicious or profane."

Walk deosil around the Circle holding the document a few inches before you, at the level of your solar plexus (where your ribs converge), and say: "I/we conjure you, Oath, to serve me/us in my/our work of parenting, strengthening me/us in wisdom, and defending me/us against malignancy, error, and fear. Receive now such virtues from the elements that I/we may be true to this purpose."

Set the document on the Altar. With Salt, make the sign of the pentagram over the Oath-writing, and say, "By the strength and perseverance of Earth be consecrated." Sprinkle or scrape incense embers onto it (if it leaves tiny scorch marks, so much the better; obviously, don't allow it to catch on fire) and say, "By the long sight and clear purpose of Air be consecrated." Drip some wax from the South candle on it and say, "By the energy and courage of Fire be consecrated." Sprinkle some holy water over it and say, "By the perfect love and perfect trust of Water be consecrated."

Hold the document to your heart and say, "To wholeness and individuality be consecrated in Spirit."

If the document has its own envelope, replace it in that envelope now, handling it as if it were an old and precious thing—for indeed it is precious, and our responsibilities as parents are as old as humanity. If it does not (yet) have its own envelope, put it carefully between the pages of your Book of Shadows. Do *not* fold it unless it was folded when you got it from the Court; if it was, refold it in the same way.

Say, "The Oath is made and consecrated. So mote it be." Gaze upon the document in its envelope or in your Book of Shadows for the space of another three heartbeats, breathe deeply together three times, and then proceed to the Cakes and Ale portion of your Circle. If your Order of Circle puts Cakes and Ale before magic, do have a sip and bite of the consecrated meal to help you ground before finishing and opening your Circle.

We don't know, and archaeological evidence has not so far hinted to us, whether surrogacy was heard of or common in original human populations. We do know that wet-nursing, fostering, and of course adoption when a mother dies, have been common arrangements for human families to make. Although adoption still has some of the associations of a taboo, in truth it is—viable, courageous, challenging, frustrating, heartbreaking and—can be, at least—ultimately very rewarding—just like any sort of parenting.

There is nothing in Wiccan theology to discourage adoption, as an alternative to abortion or as a proactive response to infertility or compelling creativity. Indeed, in Her *Charge*, the Goddess calls all acts of love and pleasure Her rituals, and asks naught of sacrifice. This suggests to us—to me and Canyondancer and to the Adventure Tradition we follow—that its time adoption came out of the closet and was recognized as yet another of the *wonder-full* options the Gods have given us to celebrate life and family.

Finally, before we close this chapter, let's remember that whether or not our families include children that we're birthing or raising, our human family includes children, and we are all children of the Goddess. With that in mind, and with thanks to the late Doreen Valiente, I give you the *Charge of the Child*:

Listen to the words of the Baby, who is known as Little One, Darling, Bibikins, Precious, My Own Sweet, and by many other names:

Whenever I have need of anything, many times in the day and night, and better it be as soon as I call, then you shall come to me and meet my need, in my distress or delight. Adore me, the future of all life. You who would learn magic, but have not yet gained the deepest secrets, look into my eyes, and there will I teach you. In unconditional love for me, you shall be truly free, and, in token of your freedom, you will love yourself as tenderly as you cradle me.

Sing! Feed me! Dance! Make music and cooing noises, all for love of me, for ours is the spirit of ecstacy, and I am the living password of perfect love and perfect trust. Keep pure my highest ideal, and let my growth neither anger nor discourage you. I am the secret door that opens upon joy; I am the Land of Youth. Suckle me from the breast or the bottle that is the Cauldron of Cerridwen and so become the holy grail of immortality.

On Earth, I give form to the spirit eternal, and beyond death, I inspire the generations. I ask much, but I am generous in return, for behold, I am an infant, and you are united in my dependence upon you, and my gurgle brings tears of joy to you in all the lands.

Now hear the words of the Young Child, in whose dust we are left in awe, whose body is miraculous yet mere beside the heart and soul and mind of youth:

I, who run barefoot over the green Earth, who turn my face in wonder to the Moon and the stars, who came from the mystery of the Waters and the desire of your heart, I call upon you to arise and take my hand, and come with me. I am the soul of Nature and bring hope to the universe. In me all things proceed, and through me all things return.

Let my oneness with all the Worlds encourage your heart to reunion. Behold: Everything you do and say teaches me more about the ritual that is life. Show me your beauty and strength, your power and compassion, your honor and humility, and approach me with both mirth and reverence.

You who seek to know me, know that all your seeking and yearning shall be to no avail, unless you shall sit down beside me and bring your own inner child to our tea table and to our games. For behold, I have been with you from the beginning, and I am that to which you shall be reborn.

Chapter Two

Between the Sabbats

No matter how many charming holiday traditions and rituals your family has, the fact remains that life is not all holidays. There are far more "everydays" on the Wheel than "holidays," and the secular Judeo-Christian culture influences those everydays. For a Wiccan family, especially one whose relatives and friends don't know about Witchcraft, it is a challenge to keep Wiccan values.

Besides "family" being differently defined now than it was even a few years ago, many other things have changed. These days, most of us work. The two-income family is the norm now, and good daycare is really hard to find and pay for. We watch more television and read less and tell fewer stories than we did 20 years ago. We send more e-mails and surf more Websites and talk less in person and by phone, and we write fewer letters. We're more pressured to accept material standards, and we're separated by more miles than we used to be. Our children face more and different dangers and challenges than many of us did when we were growing up.

Yet we practice a religion rooted in the standards of a rural, communal life that most of us never experience. How can we find and live by Wiccan values under these circumstances?

Defining our Wiccan values takes some work. We have just the one Law, that what we give into the Worlds comes back to us "threefold." We have no books of dogma, no commandments save the Rede: *An ye harm none, do as ye will.*

The "none" we may harm includes the whole of life, not just the two-foots and four-foots we call friends, and what constitutes "harm" is more than what the penal code covers. What we "will" is not necessarily the same as what we want, so our individual interpretation of the Rede can't be as simple as it looks. Our Rede and our Law make us responsible for a morality as complex and sophisticated as any on Earth.

We have other liturgical material from which we can take guidance. The *Charge of the Goddess* (see Appendix A) is rich with instruction and direction. From it, we know when to meet and what to do when we gather, and from it we can learn a great deal about why, too.

From the *Charge* we can learn what the Goddess expects of us and how to live our lives in harmony with Hers. From chants and invocations we can infer even more, for Wicca is, as Starhawk says, a "poemagogic" religion, and our liturgical material is metaphorical even when it can be taken literally.

Aphorisms like *as above, so below* guide us, too. Obviously the Earth's orbit around the Sun puts us in the universal swing of things. It's plain that similar laws of physics apply "below" as "above." But "above" and "below" aren't just two more compass points. They stand for all the expressions of duality the universe manifests, so *as above, so below* reminds us of the ultimate interconnection: Wholeness!

Perception of the God/dess' wholeness is a choice. As Wiccans, we have accepted that there is more to us than our material components, which means we accept that there is more to everything else than what we can see, too. This understanding keeps us aware and appreciative of the God/dess' work, and resistant to all the "only ways" we're urged to follow.

Wicca in the Mundane World

Doing our parental "thing," or talking to friends who ask advice, or even talking politics, we quote and interpret Wiccan "scripture" often. We include in our definition of "scripture" everything we know about the planet: geology, physics, biology, natural history, and other sciences; all the psychology and history we know; and all the various perspectives on such subjects that are familiar to us.

The more we understand about life, the less likely we are to do any harm when we act socially, politically, and magically, so we encourage each other to know as much as we can. We have always included our son when we talk about "right and wrong." We have always explained our decisions to him, told him what factors we take into account, and why some considerations are more important to us than others.

When I say "always," I mean always, too—we've talked to him about life literally since the day he was born (at home, with the help of three wonderful midwives, and yes, our insurance covered it!). Of course he couldn't understand everything we said to him at first—he still doesn't understand *everything*—but he has always known that he could rely on us to communicate. Because we do, he knows it's safe for him to share thoughts and feelings, to be honest and willing to reconsider, and to take responsibility for his own decisions.

The Explorer is an intelligent, sensitive, and responsible young man with a delightful sense of humor and good manners. We're impressed with his abilities to analyze and to empathize: he knows how to walk a mile in your shoes, and understands how hard it can be to find the best path. We like to think that our own example, guided by the Wiccan principles we've derived from the Rede, the Law, the *Charge*, and all our other liturgical material, has had something to do with his growing up to be such a great guy.

We know that being part of a coven was good for him, and that our extended "Beltane family," the couple of dozen other Witches with whom we camp, is a supportive community that stands ready to support him in need, and congratulates his successes. The city-wide Wiccan community here is wonderfully varied, and a tremendous personal and networking resource for children and adults alike.

Not every Wiccan child can enjoy such advantages today, but today's hard work will make it easier for *their* children. We are quite sure that any child brought up in the light of a Wiccan Sun and Moon will be a fine person, no matter what path s/he walks as an adult.

It's not all love among the flowers, of course; Winter is real, and so are bad days and problems. Fortunately, the Goddess' unconditional love is real, too, and a resource upon which we can all draw, whether it's manifest in the Sabbats or in the patience needed to raise children.

There are opportunities to teach and reinforce Witchcraft's world view and values. Being disinclined, for instance, to spend $25 for an evening in a loud, sticky theater to watch a violent and cynical movie, we watched a lot of PBS (public broadcasting) when the Explorer was growing up. We find that the shows on this network affirm Wiccan perspectives more often than not. (We didn't have cable then; we do now. It seems to us that all the shows are more sensation-oriented than they used to be, and it's still important to pay attention to what the kids are watching, and not take it for granted that because its on PBS or TLC or one of the Discovery Channels, it's good for them.)

Nature and *Nova* and other animal and science shows still make it clear that humanity's place is among other life forms. These shows tend to emphasize life's interconnectedness, and noticing the connections is a chance to point out that this is exactly what Wicca teaches us. Even the bits about hard science (programs about the basics of quantum physics or unified field theory, or the development of the human body within the womb, for instance) are lessons in Wicca. The scientific method has taught us nothing which cannot be expressed in Craft terms. Evolution on every scale is perfectly Wiccan, and almost everything we've ever heard on science shows can be rephrased in our religious metaphors.

Series such as *The American Experience* and *Masterpiece Theater*, various travel shows, new specials, and some of the old programs that are occasionally rebroadcast (*Cosmos* and *Connections* are two of the best) offer, at least, interesting perspectives and opportunities to talk about Witchcraft's lore and modern culture. Sometimes there's even an accurate glimpse into history!

But even the most mundane shows are opportunities to discuss Wiccan attitudes and standards—about sex, death, relationships, social obligations, matters ecological and political, and so on. The daily papers are another source of opportunity to clarify Wiccan beliefs and principles. When the Explorer was just starting to enjoy reading the comics, we found that many of the punch lines depended on a patriarchal, monotheistic perspective. References to the devil and guardian angels needed some explaining then; now, they're easy to translate.

A word about such translations and explanations: it's best, in our experience, to give children information about other religions rather than just opinions. When they're given information, our kids learn that they can rely on us to give them the facts, and to help them draw their own conclusions rather than tell them what to believe.

Many of our explanations were (and still are) historical. Moses brought his stone tablets down the mountain at about the same time as the builders of Stonehenge were bringing their stones across the plains, for instance.

Letting children know that there's an historical context for legendary events helps them realize several important truths, including the fact that history isn't one-dimensional, even if some accounts of it are. (For some guidelines as to what a child's ready to learn about the Craft and when, see *Raising Witches* (New Page Books, 2002), which was originally written as a "sequel" to *Family Wicca*, but wasn't published until several years later. We've been told it's helpful for families, for communities looking to set up Sun Day Schools—or Moon School, as we call it here in Tucson— and for people who want to reraise their own inner children to the Craft.)

The Explorer asked us many questions regarding Christianity, Judaism, and Islam that we couldn't answer satisfactorily. When that was the case, we admitted it, and went on to present Wicca's relevant thealogy or philosophy. "I can't explain why they believe this or think that," I'd say, "but I can tell you how we look at it." As often as possible, when we couldn't answer his questions, we'd ask people who could. When he got older, he read books about other the philosophies of other faiths to satisfy his own curiosity, and of course we encouraged that exploration. From us, he learned elemental Craft principles and to respect other beliefs. He's discovered what he sees as inadequacies in monotheistic dogma, but he understands that Christianity, Judaism, and Islam offer guidance and comfort to millions.

Taking this sort of sociological approach in phrasing our answers to anyone's questions (including our own) makes it clear that any philosophy that respects the Earth will develop a code of social and religious conduct that preserves the planet and its systems. Any world view that calls our physical world insignificant or unreal, or identifies it as enemy territory, is likely to generate less-considerate customs.

Why this matters is obvious, at least to Wiccans. It is better to light a candle (and honor the Moon) than to curse the darkness. But if you are so careless, foolhardy, or arrogant as to pull the wick out of your candle, what are you going to do for light and heat when the Sun goes down? A philosophy that advocates yanking the wick anyway has followers who are blinded, cold, and afraid of the dark. Wiccans (Wick-ans?) have enough sense to leave the wicks in our candles: to accept life in its entirety, rather than denying those observations and experiences that challenge us or threaten the greedy and powerful.

We talked this way to our son—still do—and to everybody else, too, for this attitude is a tool that will serve all of us well, whatever quests we undertake. Volatile issues—abortion, the death penalty, tobacco and alcohol, military expenditure and policy, education, whether or not to eat meat, homelessness, racism, sexism, and so on—need to be discussed and evaluated in Wiccan terms. Even though Wiccans hold different opinions on these subjects, your opinions and mine come from our understanding of Wiccan principles. It's those principles and our interpretation of them that we need to share with our families!

We still make a conscious effort to share the variety of Wiccan opinions with the Explorer and with others whose questions about Witchcraft we work to answer. Within each community, Witches make widely different decisions about important issues. The wonderful thing about our disagreements is that we are not threatened by them. None of the service reservists or active airmen we know argue with Circling for peace; they join us when they can. None of the vegetarians we know want to police our grocery shopping, nor do they suspect meat-eaters of sneaking flesh into the "cauldron-luck" dishes. The public Circles led by Wiccans here are joined by Druids and Asatruar and even some folks following Native North and South American paths, and their energy is always welcomed.

Witchcraft's emphasis on the interrelationships of life makes it unnecessary for us to fear or mistrust each other. There are no inconsistencies in our thealogy to put us on the defensive. The God/dess' love for us is unconditional, so ours for each other and for life can be, too.

Stuck in the Broom Closet

If your family cannot celebrate the Wheel openly, if you cannot say "Goddess" as well as "God," if your lives as Witches are bounded by community or family intolerance, then the single most important tradition your family can establish is that of *open communication*. Your children may be too young to understand everything you say, but none of us is ever too young to be nourished by the freedom that characterizes a communicating family.

How can we explain to our children that they shouldn't talk about Wicca, or about our beautiful rituals, without giving them the impression that there's something wrong about it? We think the best approach is the same one we use to teach them that their bodies are their own, not for others to touch or look at.

(By the way, one criticism I heard of the first edition of *Family Wicca* is that I didn't emphasize this point enough: that we and our children need to be quite clear that our bodies are our own, and not for others—excepting medical personnel and our choice of romantic partners—to touch or look at. Though I don't consider this a religious issue, I'll take responsibility as a priestess for assuring you that Wicca supports you and your children in being firm about those boundaries. It's up to you to pass this along to your children, to believe them and check it out if they tell you someone's gone beyond the pale, and to do something effective if you find out that it's not an innocent misunderstanding.)

All religions consider their rites sacred, most prohibit photographs of rituals (with the general exception of weddings), and most take some precautions against mockery and disruption. Even though most Americans know something about the practices of the mainstream religions, in every religion there are aspects known only to its confirmed followers. So it is with Wicca.

Our lore tells us that secrecy was once a matter of life and death; and in some places it is still a matter of life and death. Even now, some jobs (and some rental agreements, and some custody arrangements) depend on secrecy. And some of us are just not publically inclined, and wouldn't talk much about our faith even if it were mainstream. The confusion of Witchcraft with Satanism is largely resolved, but lingering pockets of determined ignorance can make Wicca's secrets seem ugly. For all these reasons, it's important that we teach our children to keep our sacred secrets.

We must also teach them ways in which they *can* talk about their religion. It doesn't always come up among children, but sometimes it does: when he was still in the primary grades, the Explorer was occasionally asked if he believed in God. For years, the Explorer answered that he believed in both a God and a Goddess. When he was a preschooler, calling the Goddess and God "Mother Nature" and "Father Time" satisfied his friends' curiosity without causing any serious misunderstandings. And these days, among teens, Wicca's positively the rage!

As the Explorer and his friends got older, I'd hear them talking about religious issues a little more specifically. Once, a neighbor child asked if the Explorer was afraid of death; as I recall, the Explorer said matter-of-factly that he wasn't, and the conversation didn't go any farther. If it had, though, the Explorer would've been able to talk about his beliefs in terms of experience, without having to argue theology. When his great-grandmother died, we encouraged him to ask questions, and we paid special attention to his speculations. We talked about what happens to flesh and bone and ether and mind, and we talked about it until he was satisfied with his understanding. (It helped me, too.)

But what about the secrets? What about those things we can't tell other people? If there's nothing wrong with them, why can't we tell?

Well, let's put that in perspective, shall we? First, there are lots of things that not everybody knows or can do. Kids, for instance, can't drive, vote, drink beer, operate heavy machinery, hold a job, negotiate contracts, get married, or gamble. In college, many classes are closed to students who haven't taken preliminary courses, and nobody suspects the upper-level classes of being bastions of crime or evil.

In more specifically religious terms, lots of churches exclude non-members from their mysteries because nonmembers are not grounded in the faith; the mysteries would have no meaning. Wiccans don't share many rituals or many pages of their Books of Shadows with noninitiates for the same reason. Noninitiates, even those studying for initiation, have not been properly prepared to understand the rites.

Wicca's mysteries are the special rewards of study and discipline. Keeping our secrets is no more "sinister" than not giving birthday presents to kids whose birthday it isn't, or not being allowed to peek to see what the presents are before the party—or not telling somebody about the surprise birthday party that's planned for her. (Most children and adults can relate pretty well to birthday party examples, so feel free to use this analogy if it works for you.)

Oh, By the Way, Mom and Dad

Although the grandparents in our family accepted that we were Wiccan, there were elements of Witchcraft they never understood (and there were aspects of their lives we didn't understand, too!). When the Explorer noticed differences in our lifestyles, he asked us about them. That gave us yet another opportunity to point out what wonderful diversity there is in the world.

No matter how well we are able to understand how someone else's mind works, none of us is responsible for the way another person thinks or acts. There's no need for any of us to be defensive about our differences.

This concept is not universal, and not everyone accepts it as true; we think it's an obvious derivation from Wiccan belief. When the Explorer did something inappropriate, we could correct his behavior calmly, without embarrassment, because we knew that he was responsible for his behavior. We knew it even when Gramma and Grampa were horrified or thought we were too lenient.

"Behold, I am the Mother of all things, and My love is poured forth across the Lands," the Goddess tells us in Her *Charge*. One of the things this passage means is that Her love is expressed in everything, even in things different from what we are and what we easily understand.

"You shall be free from slavery," She tells us, and that includes the cultural slavery of gender and status roles. "Love unto all beings" is Her law, including those beings different from ourselves. "Nor do I require aught of sacrifice," She promises—certainly not the sacrifice of our selves, though our social gods (and sometimes our families) do demand it.

Although it was from my parents that I first learned about the Pagan origins of Christian holidays, there was always much about our being Wiccan that befuddled them. They understood that Witchcraft was a revitalization of ancient ideas about humanity's relationship to life, the universe, and everything, and they understood that we're not Satanists; but they never did figure out exactly what it was we celebrated. Many folks whose grown children are Wiccan wonder the same things, and your parents might be interested too.

For people whose careers demand an almost bureaucratic conformity—at school, at work, at the club, at home, in the ladies' auxiliary—our Pagan differences are distressing. Many Wiccans have to conceal their faith from their employers and from family members, and when some of us are still persecuted violently, it's not hard to understand the concern.

Many of us grew up under The Rules (articulated a few years ago in a PBS series called *Making Sense of the Sixties*): obey authority, conceal your feelings, fit in with the group, and don't even *think* about sex. Daring to profess Witchcraft in a culture that has not significantly changed these rules—and has recently reinforced them—is scary. The only culturally acceptable way of responding to that right is to obey authority by concealing our feelings and fitting into the group. Some of our families will be angry with us if we are unwilling to atone for our "sin" of violating those rules. Some families are just worried that we, and they, will feel the wrath of...well, The Wrath.

Each family expresses these concealed feelings according to its own understanding: If you wouldn't be that way, these things wouldn't happen. No matter how kindly or gently it is whispered or gestured, this attitude presumes guilt, and that the problem is within us, not within the system. This kind of guilt is the foundation of many lives; John Bradshaw and others call it "toxic shame."

Even though guilt is not part of the Wiccan construction of the world, it sneaks into our lives on little secular feet. Our government says that individuals are responsible for a dysfunctional society, just as children are made to feel responsible for their dysfunctional parents. Refusing the yoke of guilt—deciding not to follow The Rules—can not only be dangerous, it makes *us* dangerous.

When we speak to our families about religion, we must remember that we are probably speaking to frightened people. We must reassure them in terms they can understand, in terms of the rules they've internalized. We can point out to them, for instance, that a lot of what we do looks a lot like a lot of what they do. A lot of when they do what they do comes from what we did long before they started doing it, too.

One year my parents asked me whether we celebrated New Year's Eve. "It's on the calendar," my dad reminded me, implying that if it's on the calendar, we have to celebrate it. I told him that yes, we're up at midnight on December 31st, counting down with the television, waiving noisemakers and taking pictures for the scrapbook. I did not remind him that Solstices and Equinoxes and full Moons are on most calendars, too, and that by his reasoning, the whole country should be celebrating them as well. He wasn't asking for information, he was asking to have his fear of, and for, my differences allayed.

There is so much secrecy, so many rumors and lies, that it's a wonder any of us know what we're doing. Christian holidays are so much a part of our culture that they are half-secularized, which makes it hard to tell what is religious and what is not. Some people have trouble understanding that there is more than one sort of holiday at all.

When I told my parents that our religious new year was at Samhain, they thought we were rejecting any secular celebration of the beginning of a new calendar year. Canyondancer's family thought that because we don't celebrate Christmas, we must not celebrate any Winter holiday.

As for Halloween, many people are so terrified of mortality that the idea of honoring death as a part of the life cycle is literally beyond their comprehension. Even though it is a perverted understanding, so many people understand death as an end or a punishment that facing it calmly seems, to them, insane. (You can read a little more about my Wiccan perspective on death a little later in this book; you can read a lot more about it in *In the Service of Life: a Wiccan Perspective on Death* [Kensington Books, 2003]. It's always going to be sad; doesn't have to be scary.)

Beltane's Maypole is not such a threat. Many of our parents, and many of us, can remember dancing it in grade school, and 'dancer and I both remember Maypole dances on our college campuses (mine liberal, his conservative). Even though the Maypole is straightforwardly phallic, many people's appreciations of its spiral mating dance is based on a carefully constructed and defended "innocence" of its significance.

At the same time, the Maypole is a blatant reminder of a real and significant difference between monotheisms and Wicca. Naming our flesh evil (or inferior or illusory or otherwise invalid) creates in us a schizophrenia that begs to be healed—and Witchcraft, as the button says, heals.

After his mother died, my dad said to me, "Now there's nobody between me and death." It may be the same death that separates us from our parents that reunites us with them, for our Wiccan attitude toward death—sadness without guilt or fear—allows us to comfort our elders as they face their mortality.

And as our generation of "boomer Witches" gets older, and we and our parents begin to cross the astral Western Sea on our way to the Summerland, we may be able to offer our parents (and each other) a psychological healing and rebirth in addition to the reincarnation the Gods will offer. Wicca may not be so hard for them to accept if they find its theology comforting in a moment of need: there are, as World War II vets are fond of saying, no atheists in foxholes—and monotheism isn't the only nonatheism.

There are less desperate ways of introducing parents and other family members to Wicca, of course. Scott Cunningham's *The Truth About Witchcraft Today* is an easy-to-read, nonthreatening book that many Witches have left with their families as an icebreaker.

Casual conversations offer some opportunities, too. "Isn't it interesting that Christmas celebrates the birth of the s-o-n, while Yule celebrates the annual birth of the s-u-n?" we can ask. "Did you know that eggs are ancient symbols of fertility, and people have been coloring them to celebrate the Spring Equinox for thousands of years?" "I wonder how many people know there weren't any real Witches executed in Salem?"

Almost everybody I've talked to has heard of "those caves in France," even if not everyone is comfortable trying to pronounce their name. (Les Trois Freres at Lascaux: lay twa frair at laz-coe). No one I've talked to has been inclined to call those antlered priests or the statues of "Venus of Willendorf" satanic, either, although one woman I met at a bus stop wasn't sure she agreed that there were no Christians 40,000 years ago. (Then again, on a 2003 episode of *The Tonight Show*, someone interviewed for the "Jaywalking" segment asserted that Jesus lived 500 years ago, and Joseph and Mary lived 700 years ago....)

The more we know about the history from which Wic.
better we're able to recognize and take opportunities to tell p.
truth about our religion. Some parents are still upset because the..
Wiccan children no longer practice the family religion. They may be a..e
to accept the fact that their religion, whatever it is, took one direction out
of ancient Paganisms, and that Wicca is a modern expression of the same
ancient Pagan perspectives.

As Wiccans, we know how true it is that we can choose and change
our attitudes. We also know that it is wrong to manipulate other people's
attitudes when those people haven't asked us to work with them. If you
have trouble resisting your parents' manipulations (by prayer, harass-
ment, or threat), then you can work for yourself, casting spells of protection and developing greater strength. You do not need to let them draw
you into the battles they have chosen to fight. Responses such as these
are appropriate when your family confronts you accusingly:

> "I understand that this is what you believe."

> "I am sorry that this troubles you so deeply."

> "I see that you are very upset about this."

> "I will try to answer some of your questions when we can
> talk calmly."

These responses are also appropriate when grandparents or other
relatives treat any of your children preferentially to the distress of their
siblings, or discriminate against one of your children. There are any number of reasons that children can be singled out for special treatment,
pleasant or unpleasant, and there's no reason that you, as a parent, have
to tolerate that.

Yes, of course each child will and should be treated differently: they're
all different people, with different interests and needs requiring support
and recognition. But we've all read in the newspaper advice columns about

relatives who favor one child with more gifts than the others get, or who treat one child as an outcast while including others in various activities. That's not okay, and it's your job as a parent to notice and, as discreetly as possible, let the errant relative know that it's inappropriate to act out prejudices like that.

Sometimes children will ask why Grandma or Uncle seems to hate them, or seems to like a brother or sister (or cousin) more. We think the appropriate answer is that you don't know, but that you understand it hurts your child's feelings. Sometimes people we love behave badly; sometimes they don't know the right way to express their feelings; sometimes even grown-ups don't know how they feel or why.

Unless you have the child's permission to speak on the child's behalf, though, confine your comments to the offending relative to your perceptions and feelings. "I notice that you bring Andromeda something every time you visit, and you never give Prometheus even a birthday present. I am distressed that you treat my children so unequally." Or, "I don't think you realize that this gives the impression you are angry with Prometheus, or dislike him." Following up with, "I wonder if we could talk about this," is always a good idea.

When you have to challenge someone's behavior (or attitude), it's nice to leave them a way to save face. It saves you from the error it might be to accuse someone of malice when it's only cluelessness you're looking at. If, however, the person you're talking to shows no inclination to change their offensive behavior toward your children, you're well within your rights to limit that person's interaction with your kids.

No matter what objectionable behavior you must deal with, or what objections your family raise, remember that they are scared. They interpret Wicca (and/or some other condition of your life) as a threat to their beliefs, and they may interpret your practice of the Craft as a threat to their parental power. In fact, they may perceive a Wiccan lifestyle as a devaluation of their whole lives, of everything they worked for, everything they tried to give you. With parents who absolutely won't accept Wicca, it may be best to offer affirmations of those things we do appreciate about their lives.

My mother would not articulate her religious beliefs because committing to one point of view would make her vulnerable to error, or to being proved wrong in the end. She was a world-class calligrapher, the source and nurture of my artistic bent. My father guessed he was Christian because most Americans are; a camper and fisherman, he taught me the respect for life and environment that helped me embrace Wicca.

When my father said, "If there are 100 religions, at least 99 of them must be wrong," I sometimes argued with him. "They might all be a little bit right," I'd suggest. But mostly, unless they'd heard something dead wrong about Wicca, we didn't talk about religion. They sent me clippings of the increasing number of articles they found in their paper about Pagan religions, and asked me questions if anything in those articles was unclear to them. But we didn't talk down-home and personal very often.

This is sad, as I have always been religious. I have always felt called to "the ministry," although until I found Wicca I didn't know how to answer that call. Talking about religious ideas has been one of my greatest pleasures in life, and it was deeply disappointing to me that I could not share this pleasure with my parents, who contributed more than they ever knew or believed they did.

Most of us who can't share our Witchcraft with our families would like to do so. Those of us for whom patient persistence is not a solution may feel this as a loss of nurturing, and may experience a need to grieve for it. In *Toxic Parents* (Bantam Books, 1989), authors Susan Forward and Craig Buck suggest a funeral for the expectations that our parents will never meet for us. It's a very powerful ritual, one that a solitary Witch or covener could easily adapt, and it makes the point very forcefully that we need to give ourselves a rebirth from such relationships.

As we deal with our parents' varying degrees of reluctance to accept Wicca as our faith, so must we anticipate the possibility of our children embracing a different religion when they are grown. I fantasize (still!) that the Explorer will marry a nice Wiccan girl and raise bouncing Wiccan babies—but he might not. And this has to be okay.

I first said that when the Explorer still considered himself Wiccan. Now that he's in his mid-20s, unmarried, and not Wiccan, it's seems unlikely that I'll have Wiccan grandbabies—or any grandbabies! And while I still hope it'll happen, it *is* okay if it doesn't. Mind you, I've had to work really hard to come to terms with the idea that not only is my son not (currently, anyway) Wiccan, but may not have children. I've quoted Alistair Cooke to him, about even tough times being the right time to bring children into the world, but the Explorer is not so sure it's responsible. But this *has to be* okay. It doesn't have to be easy, but it does have to be okay.

If it isn't okay with you that your kids might not be Wiccan when they grow up, if you make jokes to hide your anxiety about your kids becoming Catholics or Baptists, you need to focus on the way it feels when your parents are disrespectful of your faith and of your right to choose it.

Our opinion is that finding out the truth about our parents' religions is why we left it, and that finding out the truth about ours is why our kids will stay, or come back. Any of us could one day be on the other end of "Oh, by the way, Mom and Dad ..." but it's not something I worry a lot about. No matter which end of the phrase we draw, we need to keep in mind that love unto all beings is Her law.

Wicca at Home

Nearly everything we do at home can be done with Wicca in mind. From rearranging a room to brushing our hair, everything can be a spell. For those of us who didn't grow up Wiccan, it might seem strange, but with practice, it will seem more and more comfortable. And if we share what you might call mundane blessings with our children, it will be second nature to them.

When the Explorer was young, we got a free-standing closet in which to hang our ritual robes and store our crowns and chalices and other Tools. Of course we consecrated it before we put anything inside—but that's not all we did. Because I've always liked the idea of a private magical land behind unsuspected doors, I painted a fantasy landscape on the three inside walls and the floor of the closet.

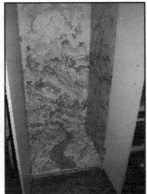

These three photos show the author's "Witch closet" closed, open to display the magical landscape painted inside, and as it looks holding various Circle accessories.

I'm not a natural (or trained!) artist, believe me. But I mixed some craft paints with some left-over latex wall paint, and got a wide range of colors. I applied these colors, lightest first, with a sponge. Later, I used some glittery fabric paint (left over from the coven banner) to tuck a castle into the painted hills.

The closet is scented, too, with the smudge we used to purify it, and with the magical scents of our favorite potpourri tucked into the corners. Our sense of smell is our most evocative, so if you decide to let one of our closets do double-duty as the gateway to a magical land, make charms out of potpourri to remind you of the magic of your youth. I used one that conjured up my grandmother's house. One caution: if you use veils, don't put them in while the scents are their strongest. Heavy scents give some people severe headaches, and because veils cover our faces, the effects can be quite distracting.

The outer face of our closet is decorated with a painted pentagram 2 feet in diameter. I haven't yet found "the appropriate symbols" to affix at the points. I particularly like Starhawk's pentagram meditations, and I was looking for just the right symbols of them, but I hadn't found them by the time we moved and thought we'd retired the closet. Now it's in my small-c craft room, holding the ritual gear 'dancer and I use now that we're practicing on our own again, and I still keep my eyes out for the right decorations.

You may need or prefer to be more subtle, but a small or hidden pentagram traced in paint or even in oil on the inside of a closet will bless it just as surely as a big copper one. (When we moved our very overt Witch-cabinet into this house, we printed a new spell of reconsecration and dedication for it, and glued it to the front of the kickspace. You can't see it unless you get down on your hands and knees, but it's there, and as far as I know, it's working.)

We first used the following Ritual of Space Dedication to consecrate a backyard ramada several years ago. One thing we learned is that it's a good idea to make more than one charm, if you're using a fabric pouch and planning to hang it outside. Our lovingly embroidered felt pouch disintegrated after a few years, and we wished we had another like it. Of course, this ritual can be adapted for any room or patio, a bed, or even the interior of a vehicle!

Ritual for Space Dedication

You will need a bowl of Salt and a bowl of Water, four candles in Quarter colors, a staff or a wand, incense and a burner, and a fifth candle of an energetic color. If you are out of doors and it is possible, don't contain the candles, but allow their wax to imbue the ground. If this is not possible, set the candles in containers from which you can recover the molded wax to use in a charm that can remain in the space.

Bless the Salt and purify the Water.

Cast a Circle as you usually do.

Hold the staff or wand over the Altar and say, "May this Altar and this place to all its corners be purified. In the name of Life and Death, so mote it be."

Everyone present repeats, "So mote it be."

Standing in the Goddess position (arms and legs outstretched) in the center of the space, say, "Blessed be, thou creature of art!"

Raise burning incense to the East and say, "May you be charged with the power of Air, and be strong and safe in the East, between the Worlds and in all the Worlds."

Raise the Quarter candle in the South and say, "May you be charged with the power of Fire, and be strong and safe in the South, between the Worlds and in all the Worlds."

Raise the bowl of Water in the West, and say, "May you be charged with the power of Water, and be safe and strong in the West, between the Worlds and in all the Worlds."

Raise the bowl of Salt in the North, and say, "May you be charged with the power of Earth, and be strong and safe in the North, between the Worlds and in all the Worlds."

Standing in the Goddess position in the center of the space, and circling slowly, deosil, in place, say, "May you be charged from the center, above and below, throughout and about, within and without. May spirit be cherished here; may you stand with strength and in safety, to be a haven between the Worlds and in all the Worlds."

Thank the Directions and the Goddess and God for making this "a safe and nice place to be." Close the Circle and let the Quarter candles burn down, if possible. Otherwise, extinguish them respectfully, save the wax for charms, and use the candles again the next time you meet in that space.

In this ritual, we placed appropriately colored candles in the corners of the area, orienting not at but as near as the corners come to the directions. By doing this, we were magically aligning the space we're consecrating with the Directions. We felt that if we put the North candle, for instance, in the middle of a wall, the space would be askew between the Worlds. We used a staff because for us a staff represents Adventure, and the spirit of adventure is at the core of our practice of Wicca. Blessing and consecrating a space with a staff means, to us, that whenever we enter that place, we are on an adventure, that puts us between the Worlds (whether we formally cast a Circle or not).

After we dedicated our ramada with this ritual, it often felt to me like a sort of magic carpet, even though it had an adobe floor. I often had visions of the whole henge, including the gardens and the pond at the West (fish and fountain and all) transported to some magical land of adventure. I was always half-surprised to find the same old kitchen inside the screen door after all.

Would I write and perform this ritual differently now, more than 10 years later? Well, yes, but not very. Since then, we've developed more Traditional invocations and blessings, and naturally I'd use those now. Back then, we were looking for simplicity, and now we appreciate a little more formality. Reviewing it for this second edition, though, I still find it quite charming—which is, after all, the point.

Here's another idea you may be able to use as we did, or adapt. The sliding door to our yard was covered with a wrought-iron barred security door. It wasn't as prison-like as "barred security door" sounds, but it was pretty ugly. There was no way to make it less blatant, so we chose to see its boldness as a strength. Let's make it a *meta*physical gate, too, we thought.

Using fairly inexpensive enamel spray paints from a hobby shop, and masking tape stencils cut with a sharp craft knife, you too can make a security door into a work of art! It might take longer than one weekend, but you can cover the door with runes and all kinds of designs—fish, cats, moons and stars, rolling hills, silhouettes of castles, wizards—whatever you like.

The runes on this portion of the "the magic gate" read, "The adventure is everything is the adventure."

You do have to be careful not to get paint on anything else—yourself or your plants, for instance. But if you use an old sheet to cover everything else, then you've got a delicately covered field from which you can go on to make many banners—two projects for the effort of one! Our Gate was so obviously decorative that most people just admired the bright colors (which fit right in with the Mexican influences here) and never noticed the religious symbols. The neighborhood kids pronounced it "funky." A success all around, we thought, so if anything such as this appeals to you, go for it!

Until O'Gaea and Canyondancer decide on a permanent place for the magic gate, it leans against a patio wall, decorated with tiny windchimes and a star ornament.

(We've moved twice since then, and only recently sold the Gate House. We'd resigned ourselves to repainting it black and leaving it for the new owners, but just before it was sold, it was broken into. The Gate held— the burglars had to take its lock out before it yielded. After it defended the place so nobly, I couldn't bear to leave it, so we had it replaced, and now it's awaiting replacement in our new yard. Some of its painted signs and symbols have faded, so we'll clear-coat it to protect the ones that are left before we set it up again.)

Spell for Transforming Anger

Sometimes something happens, to you or to somebody else, that makes you mad. Maybe a friend's husband beat her up, maybe a child got detention at school for something s/he didn't do, maybe your candidate lost the election unfairly, maybe your car stereo was stolen. Whatever it is, you're angry.

When it's something that you can't deal with directly, when the wife beater's out on bail or the car stereo's not covered by your insurance, your anger has to be directed creatively so it won't do any harm.

I've used this spell a number of times. The words vary each time according to the specific situation. Sometimes I do parts of it in my head, when I can't contain my anger until I'm home (where I can cast a Circle). If you are *able* to cast at least a minimal Circle, you'll need Quarter candles and a center candle, and appropriate incense. Unless there's a reason to use something else, I like Hecate incense for this work.

If you are working with anger you feel on someone else's behalf, be sure you have their permission to send energy to them. They're probably pretty heated about whatever it is, too, and the *unexpected* addition of your energy to theirs might not be helpful. If you can't get their permission, then just ground the energy and let God/dess decide how to use it.

Prepare and cast your Circle as you usually do.

As you light each Quarter candle, invoke the Guardian of the Direction.

Ask the Guardian of Air to clear your mind of vengeful thoughts and to clarify your perspective.

Ask the Guardian of Fire to temper your anger with determination and to help you control your magical intent.

Ask the Guardian of Water to keep you from drowning in the tide of anger, and to remind you that love is Her law, and the greatest magic.

Ask the Guardian of Earth to ground you, to connect you with firm strength, and to steady you.

As you light the incense, affirm your transportation to a space between the Worlds, where you can be calm and direct your energies helpfully. Take as much time as you need to ground and center. If your anger is extreme, do not proceed until you stop shaking or crying.

As you light the center candle, invoke the appropriate aspects of the Goddess and God.

Ask the Goddess to take the energy of your anger, transform it, and send it to the injured party for use in healing, or as a shield; or—careful, now—to the injuring party to revive his or her conscience.

Ask the God to guide the energy of your anger and direct it toward the people involved, to strengthen them or their awareness.

Ask the Goddess to transform what is left of your anger into a calm understanding that love is the law. Ask the God to transform what is left of your anger into a calm understanding that the Threefold Law is a lesson to be learned, not a vengeance to be delivered.

When the incense has burned away, extinguish the Quarter candles with thanks to the Guardians for their help. If possible, leave the center candle burning until it extinguishes itself.

In the meantime, get yourself something to eat and drink, blessing it first in your usual way. As you eat and drink, ask aloud to be nourished with love and trust. Say aloud that as the Goddess and God give you the nourishment you now take in, so you give energy to the God/dess to nourish the people you've just worked for. (Yes, you might be one of them.)

When these things are done, give yourself a few minutes of quiet time. If you feel that it's appropriate, write to the person you've worked for and let them know you've sent them energy to use as a shield against fear or injustice.

One time I used this ritual after a friend's husband had badly beaten her in the same hospital where their son lay critically injured, and I was livid. This happened several years ago, but I remember quite clearly asking the God/dess to make the abuser confront "the Guardians in the marrow of his bones" about his behavior. I thought at the time that this was okay, as far as the prohibition against manipulative magic goes, because I was certainly willing to face the Guardians in the marrow of my bones— and perfectly willing for someone to charge me with doing so if ever I started wailing on somebody else.

Looking back, I see this as more rationalization than I am now comfortable with, but I know that if ever I were that angry again, I'd probably feel the same way and do much the same thing; certainly his attitude and behavior needed confronting, and she needed an advocate. On the other hand, now I'm better at not dancing so close to what I see as the borderline between legitimate and unacceptable magic; I like to think I could channel that anger, which was absolutely legitimate, into something of more direct and immediate use to my friend.

Were I advising someone else today, I'd most likely suggest massive protection for anyone in such danger, though only with their permission; I did have my friend's permission to send magical help when I worked for her after hearing that hospital story. I would likely suggest a specific protection "fierce" enough to bounce an attacker's energy back with a bite. That would be setting boundaries and establishing consequences for their violation, rather than manipulation of anyone else's will.

Of course, there is no simple answer, or one thing you can say you "should do" every time. You have to trust your instincts, and inform your instincts, when things are calm, by becoming aware of lots of alternatives to choose from when push comes to shove. And helping our children become ever more aware of the alternatives, the ways we can temper raw emotion, is part of our job as parents.

Children haven't the intellectual or psychological maturity that complex magic requires. I don't include a "so mote it be" after the statement of their desire, and another reason for that is that...Billy has to *want* to say he's sorry (before doing magic, to encourage him to say he's sorry is okay). This mini-ritual is more to clarify and cope with child's feelings for his or her own peace of mind, not to work magic the way grown-ups do at Esbats. But children *can* raise some pretty hefty angers, and it's important for them to have a way to deal with angry feelings. A very simple ritual, that young children can do—with supervision, of course—is this:

> Stand in the middle of a Circle in which a grown-up has lit the Quarter candles. Say what makes you mad. Say how mad it makes you. Stomp up and down in the center of the Circle as you shout. When the energy level is high, fall to the ground and press your palms firmly against the floor. Let your anger leave your body through your palms. Let it go into the floor, and through the floor, into the Earth underneath. (If you have a lawn and yelling won't

alarm the neighbors, do this outside and send energy directly into the Earth!) This gives the energy of the anger back to the Mother, and has a calming effect.

Before you get up, say what you want to happen. "I want Billy to say he's sorry," or "I want Teacher to take my name off the board," or "I don't want Daddy to work late." Say how you would like to feel. "I would like to feel calm," or "I would like to feel like going to the party." Then say, "I give my anger to Mother Earth so that She can use the energy to help."

The whole ritual, including incense and food, should be supervised by an adult who does not participate. Children need to learn responsibility for their feelings, and this will help. Of course, a grown-up could use this same ritual in any situation that is too angry for rational direction of energy. We all want to have a tantrum sometimes, and this can be more effective and satisfying than throwing or breaking things

Chapter Three

Raising Children to the Craft

Some Wiccan parents are (still) reluctant to raise their children to the Craft, or even to teach their children anything about Wicca. Some families live where it's dangerous to be known as Wiccan, and the emphasis on secrecy in our lore seems to set a precedent. Some Wiccans were educated so cruelly to their parents' religion that they are alarmed by the idea of teaching religion to their children. This experience sometimes generates the argument that "it's wrong to force my religion down my kid's throat. S/he should be free to make a choice when s/he grows up."

One of our questions about that is whether any uninformed choice is really free. Another is what our children will learn about relationships if we shut them out or keep secrets. These parents, we think, need to reconsider—you don't have to teach Wicca to your kids the same way your parents' religion was taught to you. Indeed, in the years since *Family Wicca* was first published, we've talked to countless people on this subject, and addressed these and other aspects of the question of raising children to the Craft.

The neighborhood the Explorer grew up in was predominantly Gospel Baptist. His friends invited him to Sunday school a few times, and we always gave our permission. In true and natural Pagan style, he always declined to go—because "you have to get up too early."

On their part, the kids who saw me making our coven banner pronounced it "neat" without batting an eye. Cauldrons, chalices, Quarter candles—an Altar!—filled our house, and none of the Explorer's friends gave any of it a second glance.

His teachers and grade school principal had known since he entered school that we were Wiccan. I insisted that if Christian (in two languages) and Jewish songs were sung at the Winter Holiday program, "Deck the Halls" should be included as well. Indeed, the grade school called it a *Christmas* program before we pointed out that there's more than one Winter holiday. I gave teachers packets of information to clarify my requests that the green-faced, warty-nosed decorations be taken off the classrooms' October bulletin boards. And the Explorer never encountered any discrimination as a result.

A very long time ago, maybe even before he started school, an older kid taunted the Explorer about devil worship. The Explorer and two or three other children were playing in a friend's front yard, a few doors down from our house, when the older boy rode by. When he stopped, the other children looked up long enough to say, "Nuh-uh," and then they ignored him.

Almost as long ago, the Explorer took a phone call ('dancer was in the shower and I was on my way home from work) about a letter to the editor I'd written. The call was from a "fundie" (fundamentalist Christian) who told the Explorer he was being raised in a bad religion and would go to hell. By the time the caller hung up, the Explorer was in tears. It had occurred to him to hang up, but he was afraid he'd get in trouble for doing that to a grown-up. We set him straight about that right away!

Those are the only troubles the Explorer's ever had with people being aware that he was Wiccan. The car we had when he was in grade school was covered with bumper stickers, including "WITCHES HEAL" and others that made our faith obvious. Canyondancer and I both wore pentagram rings, and my necklaces were (and are) frequently visible.

Conversations the neighbors' kids overheard included words such as "coven," "Witches," "Witchcraft," "Goddess," and so on. Our rituals were sometimes overheard by our over-the-fence or across-the-alley neighbors. And our house was still, even so, the gathering place of choice for all the Explorer's friends, with their parents' blessings. In some places there would be more trouble than others, but some troubles were overanticipated. Things change—so keep your finger on the local pulse.

Unless you never speak to your kids and never do anything religiously different from your Christian family or neighbors, unless Wicca has not changed your life at all, you are raising your children to the Craft. The only question is whether you will do it with respect for your kids' intelligence and potential—or not.

Sun Day School

We are fortunate to have a fairly large and well-accepted Wiccan and Pagan community here in Tucson. The Tucson Area Wiccan-Pagan Network has, on and off for years and consistently since 2002, offered "Moon School" classes for members' children; Chandra Nelson has not only been a Moon School teacher, but developed the 2002 to 2003 curriculum. (TAWN offers adult education classes, too.) At the University of Arizona, Arizona Student Pagans still meet occasionally during the school year, offering introductory classes to the public, as well as to University students.

And Rick Johnson, a British Traditional priest has for more than 20 years offered, at least once a year, a "Wicca 101" class (a "what is" rather than a "how to" introduction to Witchcraft). Our family took the class two or three times, and now 'dancer and I are regular guest speakers.

The first time he attended, the Explorer was very young, and paid more attention to the other people taking the class than he did to the material. The second time, he learned quite a bit. If such classes are available where you live, we recommend checking them out, and for several reasons. Taking a class with Mom and Dad makes a kid feel pretty grown-up. It also lets a kid know that Wicca is not just a family tradition, but something that lots and lots of people practice.

Some of the material will be hard for children to understand, which gives you a chance to talk about the Craft in some depth and explain it in terms your children can understand. The second time we took Rick Johnson's class, the Explorer was particularly interested in reincarnation, and we had some really neat conversations about it.

Talking about these things gives you a basis for comparison: how are your family's beliefs different from others, and how are they the same? Does everyone in your family believe exactly in the same way, or are there some interesting differences among family or coven members?

When Rick realized the Explorer would be attending, he asked whether he should be concerned about the sexual references and the nudity in some of the slides he shows. I reassured him that in a Wiccan context, sex and nudity are inoffensive, and this context is, furthermore, a vital counterbalance to the dominant social attitudes, which we'll explore later.

(If there is any chance that someone in a class might fancy such pictures pornographic and be inclined to call Child Protective Services, by all means keep children from seeing such illustrations. Just realize that the legitimate reason for doing so is socio-legal, and not moral or psychological. None of the slides or photos I've seen used to illustrate points in Rick's class, or in the one or two other classes I've attended, have been not even remotely pornographic. That is, they've been very matter-of-fact, and not the least bit titillating or prurient. In my opinion, anyone who finds a skyclad ritual, or pictures of it, to be pornographic needs to get their mind out of the gutter!)

It's true that kids can be self-conscious about seeing pictures of a skyclad gathering and hearing grown-ups talk about sex. It is not true that their embarrassment or the pictures and discussions will do them any harm. Children have built-in defenses and simply don't pay conscious attention to things they can't understand.

A child's unconscious attention follows parental cues, so if Mom and Dad respond calmly, with interest and agreement, then a child's subconscious will "file" those reactions with the images and information s/he may seem to be ignoring. Years later, when adolescents want to know what to think about their bodies (and other peoples'), and need to know what attitude to take toward sex and nudity, the mental support for reverent pleasure will be there. So will support for the idea that everyone's body is beautiful and deserving of respect, no matter what its shape.

Other useful concepts will be available too; there's a wealth of information in classes like those we've been able to attend. If classes aren't available in your community (and you can't organize them yourself), then consider introducing casual lessons, perhaps from a book like *Buckland's Complete Book of Witchcraft* (Llewellyn Publications, 1986). Some of my other books—*Raising Witches* (New Page Books, 2002), and the two volumes of *Celebrating the Seasons of Life* (*Samhain to Ostara* and *Beltane to Mabon*) (New Page Books, 2004), will also be helpful for involving your children in what you do, and for working with other children in your Neo-Pagan community (as well as with your own).

(*Raising Witches* is specifically about how to organize religion classes for a Pagan community's children, and includes a curriculum and suggestions for implementing it. It was originally written to be a companion to *Family Wicca*, but at the time, the idea of "Sun Day School" was still too reminiscent of bad "Sunday School" experiences to get published. Now I am happy to recommend *Raising Witches* as a complement to *Family Wicca*.)

It's not necessary to teach Wicca by rote, although there are some things we all like to memorize. It's far more appropriate to experience

Witchcraft, to feel the wind against our faces, feel the warmth of the campfire at our feet. There are a lot of ways to bring a Wiccan education to our children, and we'll talk about some of them in the pages that follow. In the meantime, let's talk about those twin parental banes: video games and Saturday morning cartoons.

Electronic Games and Satanic Cartoons

Some 15 years ago, a book like this one wouldn't have had paragraphs like the ones your about to read—well, 15 years ago, there weren't any books like this one! When the first edition of this book was written, it was necessary to address the then-hot topic of the effects of video games and cartoons; today, it's a cooler topic, but only slightly. It was with mixed emotions that I heard approximately 10 years ago that armed forces generals were affirming that jet pilots' performances are improved by their early practice on the game keyboard. Now, it's with mixed emotions that I read newspaper articles affirming that visual acuity is improved by shooting games.

I still don't think that dropping bombs—or seeing the world as full of enemies—is a good thing for young women and men to be doing. But I do think improved eye-hand-brain coordination is good. Video games aren't exclusively war training devices; I think we can make them tools of our trade, too.

We bought the Explorer his first game set when he was five; the sets he had after that (and there have been many) he bought with his own money, saved from holiday gifts and his allowance. He understood from the beginning that buying games was up to him. The Atari we bought him came with two games; all the others he's ever owned he bought with his own money (or received as birthday or Yule gifts). To avoid spending all his money on games, he worked out trading deals with his friends, selling the games he'd beaten and buying used ones for less than half-price. From this experience, he learned about budgeting, and is now effectively frugal on all fronts.

When he was considering buying his first Sega, which had better graphics than his Nintendo, he found that it cost a fortune, and that there were fewer games available for it. He had to weigh the advantages of better graphics against the disadvantages of cost and scarcity of games, considered the fact that fewer of those games were available to rent—and decided to stick with the Nintendo a little longer. No matter his decision, he was learning a lot about value and how to make those "big ticket" purchase decisions, and the lessons have been helpful to him ever since.

As for the games themselves, yes, a lot of them involve killing an opponent. But most kids old enough to grasp the object of the game understand the rules and the powers of the "guys" on the screen, and coordinate the keyboards, are also old enough to distinguish between games and reality. If not, then parental restrictions are in order.

Many of the games are adventures loosely—very loosely in some cases—based on Western mythologies. (As I work on this revision, a *Star Wars* game was just released.) The "guys" our children move on the screen have to earn their magical tools, anticipate and avoid dangers, and use their wits as well as their weapons to defeat the enemy. Do these skills often come in handy in mundane life? If you aim to see God/dess in everyone, if you value the concept of personal responsibility, if you think general attentiveness in life, ranging from driving defensively to being an informed voter, is important, then yes, some of the skills a child learns in games can be extrapolated rather usefully.

These games can also introduce our children to magic's different logic, and, carefully interpreted, can help to lay a foundation for *real* mystical thought later on. Video games can teach kids something about cooperation, too—an attitude and skill helpful in both mundane and magical efforts.

In fact, the time the Explorer's friends spent playing video games was time they got to hear peer congratulations and to be part of a winning team. When games offer a chance to escape the too-low or too-high expectations parents and teachers may have of a child, and the chance to succeed at something that matters to the child, that's magic—no matter how mundane the popcorn we clean up afterward.

Sometimes we found the Explorer already familiar with a concept we wanted to teach him—through his video games. The use of magical language, for instance, or the idea that roughly similar rules may change slightly from game to game, ritual to ritual, or astral plane to astral plane. We also found "game reality" a useful analogy when trying to make points he might not otherwise have understood.

Sure, I got sick of hearing the bleepity-bleep of video games, but when I saw a group of 10- and 11-year-old boys playing in teams, making next-step decisions by consensus, sharing hints and helping each other's "guys" stay alive, was I going to *complain*? Not when I could look out the window and see Bloods and Crips milling in the street like cattle. Not when the nightly news presented people arguing that it's everyone for themselves as far as food and shelter and medical care go. Gang menace may have diminished some since then, but it seems to me that the everyone-for-themselves mentality has become more entrenched, so I'm grateful for the standards—the expectations—of cooperation my son learned from his video games.

Just recently, at least one game has been taken off many store shelves because, as it turns out, there's a "code" players can download and use to access "sexually explicit" material. Now, I haven't seen or even heard this "explicit" material described in a way that lets me decide whether I think it's pornographic or not, but I am displeased that manufacturers are willing to sneak material into games, no matter how difficult it might be for inappropriate audiences to see it. On the other hand, even if we know about such "bonus material" and choose not to allow those games in our own homes, that doesn't ensure our kids won't play them—and access the naughty bits—somewhere else.

Truth in advertising is a good thing, but censorship is not a way to protect our children from products not advertised truthfully. The way we can help our children in this regard is the same way we can help them cope with other aspects of their lives: by being honest with them ourselves, by acknowledging our own values, and by showing them how to evaluate what's going on around them. It may be easier to call for investigations and try to blame "the media" for everything we don't like, but it's not constructive—and perhaps ironically, it's not honest.

Video games were never my choice for recreation, and I don't have to play them, but our children need to have the freedom to develop confidence in their own choices. Our job is not to teach them *what* choices to make, but *how* to make appropriate choices! We will be more successful at raising "good guys" if we respect their right to make different choices than we would—though it's our obligation as parent-regents to help them inform their decisions. The Goddess' love is poured forth across the Lands, and is manifest even in video games; I think that if Wiccan parents listen carefully, they will be able to hear Her voice even in the bleepity-blips and zings, bangs, and crashes.

As for cartoons, they've changed since the Explorer was young. I remember shows like *Rainbow Bright* and the *Smurfs* being called Satanic; more recently, Jerry Falwell accused poor ol' Tinky Winky on *Teletubbies* of being gay and a corrupting influence on very young children. Golly! If your kids don't watch cartoons at your house, they probably catch them on somebody else's television at least once in a while. Like the fundies who abhor them, there's really no way to avoid them completely.

We share a national concern that the violence riddling many cartoons and other children's shows desensitizes our kids and substitutes a dangerous unreality for the truth of assault. Lately I've read reports of a few studies that show that these exposures don't make our children more violent (though there seems to be evidence that day care does, for a number of reasons). The Explorer never watched shows that overtly glamorized combat, and never bought or was given the play figures that went with those shows. He found a G.I. Joe figure or two, usually with an arm or a leg amputated; I thought it was fitting that the few war dolls he had were maimed.

Problems are present even with the best cartoons, of course. In the Explorer's day, it was the Smurfs: there were 100 males and only one female, and they were of necessity patriarchal. But Mother Nature was their patron, their only enemy was an incarnation of greed and exploitation, and they did careful magic in self-defense. *He-Man* was a favorite for a long time. The parallels to our Pagan world view were often useful. Although male characters dominated the show, the few females were their equals, and later, She-Ra got her own show. The Explorer appreciated the moral points He-Man made at the end of each episode, and so did we.

Then there were the Teenage Mutant Ninja Turtles—after one of whom our son named one of our cats!—whose show was rather overtly Pagan. I haven't watched it lately, but understand that it's still on TV.

Because these shows were not set in the real world, the fighting he saw in them did not seem, to the Explorer, to be modeling real-world behavior. Other cartoons, purporting to take place in the real world, contained confusing violence. Even so, my worry was never that the Explorer would be misinformed about firearms or flamethrowers, but that he would accept the *relationships* such shows posit.

Not only are personal relationships poorly modeled in many children's shows, but the relationships among social classes, between governments, between citizens and governments, and the relationship between "civilization" and nature are also unrealistically presented. The Explorer sometimes watched *Captain Planet*, which was an exception. It was about an international team of young characters, each contributing an elemental power bestowed by Gaia for the as-needed creation of the title's superhero. Though it was not a bad little show, it is no longer on the air now (except maybe in syndication).

One must expect most cartoons to be one-dimensional, of course, like any other half-hour- or hour-long television show that exists primarily to make money for its sponsors. Cartoons weren't and still aren't any worse than 90 percent of the live-action shows broadcast. It's just that they're more often watched without supervision, so that their subtle fictions—and their commercial messages and the standards *they* establish—go unchallenged.

Like your children are or will be, the Explorer was able to notice that most real families are different from television families. But the premises in cartoons are disguised in animated fantasy landscapes, and can sneak into the subconscious minds of children who aren't yet "hip." We don't think that a ban on television is a reasonable solution, though some families do. We figure that banning television, or setting arbitrary time limits on watching, is as much a cop-out as letting kids watch anything they want. A moderate course, though it takes more time and effort, seems more responsible to us.

Watch what your kids are watching. You don't have to sit with them all of the time, but know what they tend to watch, and if you have objections, tell your kids why. Even if the child is too young to understand your explanation, explain anyway. If what you're saying doesn't register, the fact that you *are* explaining eventually will, and you won't have established a pattern of overpowering your kids just because you're bigger or louder. (The fact that you explain your decisions to your children doesn't mean your decisions are negotiable, though if their counterpoints are valid, you should consider them. You should be guiding them from authority, rather than from sheer power. Explanations may sometimes be put off, but should never be unavailable.)

Remember, too, that children have different tastes than adults, and that children of different ages enjoy different things. Each of our children is an individual: some things that frightened his friends seemed just silly to the Explorer; some of what he thought was cool was atrocious to them. From the black-and-white television we sometimes let the Explorer watch in our bedroom, we could occasionally overhear the laugh track of *America's Funniest People* over the pauses of whatever we were watching on PBS—and that was okay.

Hearth's Gate priestess Chandra Nelson homeschooled her daughter, Ivy, before enrolling her in a public school, and still supervises the 8-year-old's television experience. Here's some of what she has to say about children's television in the 21st century.

"I'd say that I've relied on television as a schooling resource very little. [Watching television] is a very passive experience; I prefer a more interactive approach. However, there are certain shows we watch together and discuss for homeschooling.

"There are very few shows that she's allowed to watch that she can't watch on her own. She knows which shows are allowed and doesn't watch anything else without permission. I always watch shows with her for at least the first three times, and intermittently thereafter. And I am always within hearing distance when she watches TV."

My son's 26 years old now, so it's been a long time since I watched children's TV. As I've said, in the Explorer's day, most of the shows that we could relate to Paganism were cartoons. That's changed at least a little bit, with shows like *Teletubbies*, *Bear in the Big Blue House*, and *Little Bear*.

Chandra says she finds "most young children's shows to be Pagan friendly because they generally teach compassion, problem-solving skills, empathy, and diversity. Disney's *Bear in the Big Blue House* and Nick Jr.'s *Little Bear* have had episodes that celebrate the Solstices, Equinoxes, Harvest festivals, and the Moon. Bear, in *Bear in the Big Blue House*, talks to his good friend, Luna, the Moon, every day about his daily experiences. Little Bear's community celebrates Yule with fairies and bonfires, and he has a friend who may or may not exist who's a mermaid."

These are her two favorite shows for the 3- to 6-year-old set. She says that "also for this age group there's *Sagwa, the Chinese Siamese Cat* on

PBS, which teaches some things about ancient China and is a lovely show besides. *Dragon Tales*, also on PBS, is full of magic."

And for older kids? "For the grade-schoolers there's a great show on Toon Disney, *Recess*. The third-grade teacher character says such things as 'Oh, my Goddess!' and 'Alright, now, class, let's all take a deep breath and find our center.'

"Not quite as overtly Pagan, but very funny, and with a Pagan flair is another Disney offering, *Dave the Barbarian*. While Pagan themes abound in the show, you may have to point them out to your child between the guffaws." And, she says, "On Discovery Kids, *Tutenstein* gives a health dose of Egyptology on the grade school level."

For older youngsters, "the preteen to teen bunch," as Chandra puts it, "Discovery Kids' *Truth or Scare* looks at the myths and facts of many different New Age and Pagan subjects. Their show on witchcraft was very well done. Another Discovery Kids' show worth mentioning is *Strange Days at Holsey High*. This science fiction show often deals with topics that could lead to a Pagan discussion."

Chandra continues: "Our favorite shows have rather obvious reference to Paganism (obvious at least to a Pagan). If something is done differently than we do it, we discuss why, and we sometimes incorporate some of it into our own celebrations. Even on overtly Christian shows (the overt Christianity usually shows up around Christmas) Ivy has seen correlations to what we do."

I think it's true that there are more Pagan-friendly shows on now than there were 20 years ago, and we Pagans aren't the only ones noticing, either. I've seen quite a few articles lately about the "liberal" and "anti-Christian" bias in the media. In fact, I notice more overt Christianity in shows than Chandra and her family do—maybe because I watch more television. Just this afternoon, for instance, I saw the beginning of an episode of *Sabrina the Teenage Witch*, in which Sabrina was preparing to celebrate...Christmas!

But beyond the rich opportunities Judeo-Christian holiday customs offer to television and movie writers around the Winter holidays, I see a lot of monotheism in TV shows. "Oh, God," or "Omigod" is an oft-uttered line. People talk about going to church and Sunday school. Ministers are invited to dinner. The Bible comes up now and again, in references ranging from its moral authority to the record some people keep in their Bibles of family genealogy. Some would say these are secularized references, but no one denies that the God of "Omigod" is the Judeo-Christian deity, and even when the church's or minister's denomination isn't specified, everybody "knows" it's a Christian one.

Right-wing Christian conservatives complain because many of the references to God and religion are "negative." Of course, they're counting references in comedy routines, which wouldn't be comic if they weren't negative. Wicca's *Charge of the Goddess* commands us to keep "mirth and reverence" with us, but that's a foreign and offensive idea to fundamentalists. But I digress; I mean to be talking about children's television, not the childish attitudes of some people who watch it.

It's okay that your children like to watch different things, read different things, listen to different music, and eat different foods than you do, as long as you know what they're doing and know it isn't hurting them. Take some time to watch the shows they enjoy with them now and then, and take the time to talk about those shows. Try to appreciate the show from your child's point of view if you expect your child to appreciate your opinion.

Of course, neither video games nor television shows can be allowed to get in the way of real life. Mealtimes and bedtimes and homework and playing outside and family activities are all more important. Be sure that those things are available to your children. It is unrealistic to expect a child to remember to break for dinner or to end an exciting game to go to bed; and if we keep the television on for news while we're at the table, a kid's going to think it's just as reasonable to keep it on for something s/he likes to watch.

Even the worst shows can spark interesting family discussions, as long as we don't take our kids' choice of entertainment personally. (Remember, our senses of humor change!) Children sometimes watch shows to have something in common with their friends, and we chose to let the Explorer watch a couple of stupid shows—which we could talk about—rather than allowing him to engage in other behaviors children *do* to feel like their part of a group. We asked questions like these:

- ► "What would happen if a kid really did that in school?"

- ► "How would it feel if one of your friends played that joke?

- ► "Have you been to a house that looks like that?"

- ► "I wonder how much money clothes like that cost?"

- ► "Have you ever seen anyone get shot? Let's watch the news and see if we can figure out what that would be like."

If we are sensitive to our children's developmental needs, we'll be able to help our kids meet those needs in healthy and creative ways. Kids need to know themselves as individuals, separate from their parents and on the way to independent adulthood, and they need to check out what other people's attitudes are like. We need to support them in this quest, even if means sitting through a rerun of *The Cosby Show* one more time.

So, when the shows your kids watch and the video games they play drive you up a wall, remember that *we are God/dess*, and make an effort to show your children the faces of the Gods in whatever they're watching.

Symbol and Metaphor

The Explorer never memorized the *Charge* or the *Witches' Rune* (though I think he knew our Quarter calls), but all of our liturgical material was familiar to him. He recited bits of it in Circle for years. He still knows a few chants, and he knows what to expect of Sabbats and Esbats, whether he's present for them or not.

Children develop the capacity for symbolic thought—metaphor—somewhere between the ages of 8 and 11. It's not beyond a child of that age to understand that no, there isn't a big Lady in the Sky, but that the spirit of life is like a mother to everything.

The Explorer's first models for the Goddess and God were Mother Nature and Father Time. Father Time is not, strictly, a Wiccan figure, but he embodies the ideas of mortality and natural cycles, and he is a nonthreatening figure in the non-Pagan world. Though most of Wicca's rituals emphasize the God's youthful aspects, it's important to remember that the Sage is also God-like. Men, thankfully, do not all die in their prime, and we need male as well as female role models for our elderhoods.

The Wiccan world view draws on thousands of years of history interpreted through personal experience, and Wicca tends to explain the world in terms of personal experience. Here's an example of what I mean:

When the Explorer was about 4 years old, we went early to a site to see the city's Fourth of July fireworks. While we were waiting for the main display, he spotted a few backyard fireworks, bottle rockets, mostly, shooting into the deepening dusk. He thought those wobbly red streaks were what we'd come to see. They were cool, we acknowledged, but nothing to what would start in a few minutes. When the city display went off, the child was absolutely amazed.

The next summer, we went to Disneyland. We told the Explorer about the theme park's Electrical Parade and fireworks. "Disneyland's display will make the Fourth of July look like backyard fireworks," we said, preparing him ahead of time. He couldn't imagine what the Disneyland 'works would be like, but he understood the metaphor—and he wasn't disappointed, either.

Now, years later, we still compare anticipated experiences to things we've already done using the "Disneyland fireworks" example, and even when what we're looking forward to is beyond his capacity to imagine (though not much is, now), he can get some idea what to expect. After that summer, we always said that Life makes Disneyland's 'works look like backyard fireworks—and we don't think he's been disappointed yet. (To tell you the truth, we think that the Summerland, the experience that awaits us beyond death, will make the D'land fireworks look like bottle rockets. Obviously we can't say exactly how, but we don't expect to be disappointed.)

What's the Younger Generation Coming To?

The Explorer's friends shared lots of "information" about the ways of our world and the ways of the human body. Taking even the most impossible religious legends to be literally true, many of these children had some trouble distinguishing fact from fiction; the Explorer made his own evaluations, and then shared them with us.

When I was writing the first edition of *Family Wicca*, he was old enough to draw on his own experiences to answer many of his questions about other religions, and about the conclusions his friends were drawing from their dogmas. Of course, we'd been explaining the world do him in terms of his own experience, too, same as you're doing with your kids.

The Explorer understood, early on, that all religions are trying to answer the same questions he was asking back then. He accepted at an early age that every religion phrases its questions and answers differently. We think it's really important for Wiccan parents to give their children the opportunity to compare personal experience to thealogy and draw their own conclusions. This is the most appropriate way to teach the Craft; and after all, that's how many of us came to Wicca, isn't it.

Children can be grounded in Wicca very gently. Notice how good the bath water feels at the end of the day; make it feel better with herbs. Notice how good it feels to take a deep breath when you watch the sunrise. See how a candle or a crackling fire is hot and bright like the Sun. Aren't rocks like mountains, maybe the northern mountains? Isn't it cozy and safe under the bedcovers, dark like a cave deep in the Earth? Isn't it neat that sometimes when you're thinking about somebody, they call or you get a letter from them? Or that sometimes when you want something special for dinner, you come home and that very thing is almost ready?

The Goddess gives abundant opportunities to lay a humanist foundation upon which our children can build a Wiccan faith. What stands out in our experience as different from what we learned can be what our children experience as the norm. Blessing the bread at dinner. Libations. Quarter candles. Attention to the phases of the Moon and the Sun.

Recycling and other environmentally sensitive habits. Lateral thinking and consensus decision-making. Attention to passage through life's stages, with respect for all of them. Appreciation of religious and cultural differences. The common ground of community involvement. Respect for each other's feelings.

There are a number of very good books about raising children. We're not talking about books that tell us what to do, although most good ones give helpful examples. We're talking about books that give us the kind of information we need to decide for ourselves what to do in various situations. We need to know how, and in what stages, human brains develop from infancy. We need to know which developmental skills are indications of readiness for what sorts of experience. We need to understand the ways that children of various ages are likely to express certain needs so we don't misinterpret their behavior. (My own *Raising Witches* is just such a book for Neo-Pagans, written from our Wiccan perspective but easy enough to "translate into" Druidry or Asatru.)

When we were pregnant, 'dancer and I read all the books we could get, and believe me, we took a lot of ribbing from our friends. "Are you going to raise the baby by the book?" they'd ask snidely. "Parenting is just natural," they'd say, and "kids aren't machines."

No, they're not. But they aren't miniature adults, either; the developmental stages they go through are both delicate and critical. *Homecoming* (Bantam Books, 1990) is a book John Bradshaw wouldn't have needed to write if raising children were a cinch. It's about healing, reclaiming, and "championing" your wounded inner child. Our inner children—Starhawk says "younger self," Jung says "wonder child"—are wounded by ignorance and insensitivity to basic developmental needs.

Some of the books we found very helpful are listed here, but this isn't a comprehensive list. It doesn't even include all the books we read and relied upon, because we've cleaned out our bookshelves more than once since then. But they are books we recommend as being useful and compatible with Wicca.

► Boston Women's Health Collective, Inc. *Our Bodies, Ourselves* (Simon and Schuster; we read the 1973 edition, and you should get the most recent.)*

► Boston Women's Health Collective, Inc., *Ourselves and Our Children* (Random House; we read the 1978 edition, and you should get the most recent.)

► Bradshaw, John, *Homecoming, Reclaiming and Championing Your Inner Child* (Bantam Books, 1990)

► Smith, Lendon H., M.D., *Children's Doctor* (Prentice Hall, 1978; if there's a more recent edition, get that.)

► Smith, Lendon H., M.D. *Improving Your Child's Behavior Chemistry* (Pocket Books, 1984; get a newer edition if there is one.)

► Sousa, Mrs. Marion, *Childbirth at Home* (Bantam Books, 1977.)

*My writer friend April reminds us that until the 1998 edition, *Our Bodies, Ourselves* touted abortion as the appropriate alternative to "keeping the baby." Interpretation is apparently not a strong point—even the 1998 edition devotes a 17-page chapter to abortion and only two pages to adoption. The anatomical illustrations are helpful though.

Remember, when any of these books say that "magic" or "magical thinking" is pretend, superstitious, and so on, they're talking about *fairy-tale magic*, not what *we* do; don't let that turn you off. Kids are more important than semantics.

And in some communities, we Neo-Pagans are lucky enough to find children's programs. Where I live in Arizona, the Tucson Area Wiccan-Pagan Network has a Moon School up and running for several years now. Last I heard, there was also a group addressing children's needs in Albuquerque, New Mexico. If there's nothing like that where you live, maybe you can help get something started.

Some Projects for the Family

A great way to teach Wicca gently and to demonstrate Wiccan respect for the family unit is to work on projects together. Most Wiccan families are already recycling, everything from aluminum and glass, to the clothes we give to (and buy from) our local thrift shops. Many of us are already participating in local environmental efforts—here, in May of 2003, the Tucson Area Wiccan-Pagan Network "adopted" the public park ramada where we've been meeting for more than a decade, and which members keep clean. Some of us are politically active and our children march or help at mailing parties with us. Some of us are able to circle publically, too.

All of these activities are wonderful family experiences, but even those of us who are publically inclined and "out of the broom closet" like to do some family things together at home. Here are some ideas we like.

Calendars! Everybody needs one. One of Tucson's High Priests used to make them for his friends, with drawings he collected over the years. Any of us can illustrate wall or desk calendars; it's especially easy with templates offered in several computer programs. Another calendar that's fun to make is an advent calendar. Most of us associate advent calendars with the days leading up to Christmas, but we can make them for our own holidays, too. Between any two Sabbats, for instance, it's fun to open the "little paper doors."

We used to open one between Mabon and Samhain. Outwardly, it was a steaming cauldron; under the doors were all kinds of Pagan images. For the longer periods of time Pagan advent calendars cover, you might use paper larger than standard notebook size.

Collect several pictures—draw them yourself, clip them from newspapers, magazines, or catalogues, from advertisements that come in the mail, or use the clip art on your computer program. You'll need one picture for every day on the advent calendar. If young children want to contribute their art, try making your calendar on poster board. Someone old enough to use a craft knife will need to do the cutting, but poster boards are both big enough to take larger drawings, and sturdy enough to last several years.

When you have enough pictures, decide on art for the front of the calendar. Draw it colorfully on paper the same size as the page or poster board that will hold all of the pictures you've collected, and be sure to leave lots of room to cut the "little paper doors." Finally, arrange the pictures on the backer to match the pattern of windows on the cover sheet, and glue the pictures down. Then, after you've cut each paper door on three sides (so it can be folded open), glue the cover drawing on top of the picture page.

Use a very thin line of glue at the outer edge of the cover page, so you don't accidentally obscure a picture. If you aren't using poster board, you'll need to mount the whole calendar on stiff cardboard. We used a picture-frame back, one with a built-in tripod, so we could set our finished calendar out on a shelf.

Trimmed with ribbon or glitter, or even shells or stones, these calendars can last for years and become favorite holiday decorations. At the same time, they teach a family to focus on Witchcraft's symbols, anticipate Wiccan holidays, and remember the common ground we share with other Pagan faiths.

Making coloring books is also fun. Drawing pictures of Sabbat and Esbat celebrations is a cozy way to fill up rainy hours if puddle-stomping isn't practical. If you want to use coloring books as gifts, you can photocopy the original pictures and ask your local copy shop to pad them with cover pages and card stock backs. Once that's done, it's easy to separate the individual books. Of course, if you want to draw enough original pictures for several coloring books, that's great too. Depending on how specifically Wiccan your pictures are, these coloring books might make nice donations to local children's shelters and hospitals. Wrapped in tissue paper with a small box of crayons, they're hours of fun.

Here's an example of a page made from clip art in the Print Shop program. You could make similar pages by tracing pictures from magazines or calendars. There are also some Websites that feature downloadable pages, and you can find them by entering key words in your browser.

DO YOU CALL THIS SABBAT BRIDE OR IMBOLC?

This coloring book page was created with clip art and includes a caption; yours might be hand-drawn and without words.

Brooms can be made in a variety of ways. You can look for straight, slender fallen branches and tie a collection of stiff twigs to one end, or you can make one with good old construction paper. Use a tightly rolled tube for the handle of the broom. Wrap a shorter piece around one end, and cut fringe for the besom. You can even use it to sweep project scraps off the table!

Banners can be much less complicated than what you'd make for a coven; they can be easy to make with glue, scissors, and several sheets of construction paper. Family coats-of-arms are also fun to design and make. Sabbat and Esbat coats-of-arms can turn into wonderful decorations, and help teach seasonal correspondences as well.

Greeting cards, very expensive in stores, and fun to do on a computer, can also be handmade. They can be fancy or folksy, with little more than scissors, glue, and the ever-popular construction paper. Stickers from craft stores, paper doilies, ribbon scraps, glitter, sequins, markers, crayons, confetti—all these things will personalize the cards and stationery you can design and make.

What else can families create together? Well, with knitted, crocheted, or tatted doilies (that you make yourself or find at a thrift shop) and a length of ribbon, you can make gathered pouches. These don't require any other materials, although a large safety pin (diaper pins, if you can still find them, work well) attached to the end of the ribbon makes it easier to thread through the edge of the doily. If you enjoy hand sewing or have a machine, you can make fabric pouches; an advantage to these is that you can cut them to shape. We've made quite a few pouches of various sizes with felt "squares" (they're really rectangular), too. They'll hold an assortment of things, from a deck of Tarot cards to athames or other Tools.

Something families can always do together is play games. We can play word games, for instance, almost anywhere—in the car, on a hike, in a waiting room. *I'm Going to the Moon* is an old favorite of ours. It's an alphabet game, and can very easily be played as a Wiccan alphabet game. Here's how it might sound:

First player:	I'm going to the Moon and I'm taking...an athame.
Second player:	I'm going to the Moon and I'm taking...an athame and a bolline.
Third player:	I'm going to the Moon and I'm taking...an athame, a bolline, and a cauldron.

First player again: I'm going to the Moon and I'm taking...an athame, a bolline, a cauldron, and Doreen Valiente!

Each player repeats the growing list of luggage and adds an item—or a person—that begins with the next letter of the alphabet. (The late Lady Doreen could go as a "d" or a "v.") For each game you play, you could assign a theme—Witches Tools, magical places, magical beasts, and so on.

My Grandfather's Cat is another alphabet game, a little more complicated than I'm Going to the Moon. The first player says, "My grandfather's cat is an *awful* cat who *acts* like an *ape*." The next player doesn't have to remember any of the "a" words, but describes the cat with "b" words. In each description, there has to be an adjective and a noun; the third letter-word can be a verb or an adverb, or another adjective or noun. "My grandfather's cat is a finicky cat who flies and plays the flute," you might say; perhaps your grand*mother*'s cat is a wonderful cat who waves a wand. Or it might be the High Priest/ess's cat!

If your family enjoys board games, and the kids are old enough, try Witches' Scrabble. It follows the same rules as the standard game, but you keep the words you spell related to the Craft, or to a particular Sabbat, or to another Pagan theme.

Now and again, in a cowan catalogue, you find games that are almost Wiccan; the still-growing New Age consciousness has contributed much in this respect. We recently found a game called Go Goddess (see *www.gogodess.com*). Its objective is to "allow women the opportunity for growth and personal empowerment through discovery, support, and the sharing of themselves and their individual outlook—with other women." There's a girls' version, too. The Internet reveals several sources for cooperative card and board games. Some Tarot decks include instructions for games, and encouraging a child to tell his or her own stories about the images on the cards, even before s/he learns their traditional interpretations, will be fun for everybody.

Chapter Four

Magic

$\mathcal{M}$agic at its most basic is energy collected from life's reservoir, shaped, and directed toward a goal. Wiccans work magic in particular ways, with certain words and gestures, because over generations, these forms have acquired the power of our understandings-in-common. There are at least as many ways of working magic as there are cultures and religions in the world. Wicca doesn't use all of them, but Wiccans can use almost any!

Formal Witchcraft—full Circles, Traditional forms, precise liturgies—raises power through adults' minds. Children who are not yet familiar with or "fluent in" the cultural sources of Craft rituals don't draw the same strength from them. But magic has been in the world longer than even the customs our rites draw upon, and children can bring their energies to magical work even if they don't work like adults. Don't discourage your kids from raising and directing energy just because they can't do it the same way you do.

Within Wicca's basic symbolic framework (see Appendix B), let your children make their own magic. You'll be able to introduce them to the formalities later; when they're young, it's more important to develop their confidence and to integrate magical work into their lives so it doesn't seem unreasonable to them later. Our son now understands the effects of magic in psychological terms, which is fine: magic works through many mechanisms, and human psychology is one of them.

As soon as your child is old enough to manage the concentration, you can give her or him some visualization exercises. Work with your child's natural inclination, and to validate his or her own experience. In early exercises, let the child choose the image s/he wishes to visualize.

Guided meditations are good for children. Of course, before you use one, you need to make sure you'll be uninterrupted, and that the child knows you'll stop if anything frightens her or him (even though you'll be as careful as you can to make it not frightening at all).

If you can't find or afford an appropriate one (on tape or paper) in a local occult shop or in a catalogue, make your own. Write your own empowering script, describing places your child knows and loves. Choose soothing music and read your script into a tape recorder while the music fills the background. Speak softly, slowly, and clearly. Stop speaking for anywhere between 10 and 30 seconds whenever there's something for the listener to "do" in the meditation. (Practice first to get the right timing, and a good sound balance of the music to your voice.) Here's a meditation I wrote for the first edition of this book; many people have said they enjoy it enormously.

The Cave of Many Colors

Imagine yourself lying on a soft, fresh-smelling grassy place in a quiet, sunny wood. The sun is bright and golden, shining through the green, rustling leaves. Feel the gentle wind touch your face, softly, like Mother's fingers. Relax. Relax your whole body. Just relax, just let go; trust the Earth.

You are comfortable lying on the grassy forest floor. Just relax. See the patterns the sun makes in the branches above, and just relax. Smell the earth, smell the trees, feel the wind. Feel the sunshine and the shadows, and just relax.

Let yourself sink deeply into the soft grass; let it hold you. Feel it beneath you, feel it cradling you, and just relax. Feel it hold you. Trust the Earth and just relax. The sun is warm, the breeze is gentle, the grassy ground holds you, and you are very comfortable.

Feel the grassy ground beneath you. Feel it under your heels, under your ankles and calves. Feel the Earth, safe and secure, holding you like your mommy, holding you, cradling you like the womb. Feel it holding your hips, your back, your shoulders, your neck. Feel the Earth support your hands and your wrists and your elbows and your arms. Feel the Earth support you and relax, just relax. Just relax and enjoy yourself. Feel good.

You are supported; you are embraced. You are relaxed, you are safe and secure. You are lying in a beautiful, soft, sunny, grassy forest clearing, blue sky above you. The sun is shining softly through the branches. You're safe and comfortable, and you have no cares, no worries. Just lie and enjoy the comfort, feeling the wind and smelling the grass and the leaves.

Feel the sun on your face, hear the wind in the trees. Feel the grass beneath you, the coolness and the moisture. Hear the birds singing. Hear them rustling on the forest floor. Listen to the squirrels running through the branches above you. Listen for the woodpeckers and the hummingbirds. Just relax and be aware of this place. Relax and be right in the middle of this clearing, safe, and quiet, and comfortable.

⋇ *Pause* ⋇

It's such a nice clearing, such a beautiful place, so warm, so full of sound and smell and color and life...You're very comfortable, very safe and secure, very relaxed. And now, with no effort at all, you rise up and move, as fast or slow as you like, across the clearing. You move easily across the clearing to a place where the woods meet the edge of some rocky foothills. And hidden among the rocks, you find a small, secret cave.

≼ Short Pause ≽

This is your cave, yours alone. No one else has ever seen it. No one else knows it's here, or what it looks like. It's yours alone, and it's a safe cave that pleases you. You look inside the cave and feel the breeze coming from it. You see a shaft of sunlight coming down between the rocks that make the ceiling of the cave.

This sunlight is warm and peaceful—and it's your sunlight. The secret cave with its earthy floor and the beautiful shaft of sunlight is yours, and yours alone. It's quiet and peaceful and safe, a special, secret place.

You step inside the cave, and it is dark and cool; you feel at home here. The sunlight coming through the roof is like a golden rainbow. It is warm and beautiful and you want to touch it, to feel it. You step forward and you are standing in the shaft of sunlight. You can feel the warm sun on your face, and the bright light makes you squint a little bit. You feel alive, tingling with life. You are safe, and you are relaxed and comfortable.

You are alert, and you notice every detail of your cave. The earthy floor is almost white where the sunlight touches it. You can see the dust dancing, swirling upward in the warm sunlight. The bits of dusk sparkle like diamonds against the dim walls of the cave. You reach out and touch the dark, cool walls. The palms of your hands caress the stone. Feel the rock beneath your fingers. Feel its texture, the cracks, and the mosses. Feel the curving rocks, feel how solid they are. Lean against the walls. You are safe here, safe and comfortable and relaxed.

⤙ *Short Pause* ⤚

Stand in the shaft of sunlight, and see it light your hands as you hold them up to the sunshine. Move your hands in the light. Watch the dance of light and shadow on your hands, and feel it on your skin. Close your eyes and turn your face up toward the light, and feel it touch you. Feel the light stroke your face. Feel the sunlight. Your hands are still dancing in the light. Watch them, and see that the light is turning red. See all the different colors of red that there are. See them dance on your skin. Feel them. Feel the red touch you.

Red is life, red is love; red is safe and secure. Red is the color of blood, and you can feel the blood in your body. You can feel your heartbeat in this red light, feel it pumping life through your body. Feel the strength of life, and see its beauty in the red light.

⤙ *Pause* ⤚

Now see the light change to orange, and feel the orange light on your hands. See all the different colors of orange that dance on your skin. Feel the orange colors within you; feel them all through your body. Feel the orange all around you. Feel it in the walls of the cave. Feel it all over.

⤙ *Pause* ⤚

Watch the sunlight turn to yellow, bright yellow. Feel yellow touch your skin, and see all its different colors. Feel yellow's energy dance within. See it on the walls, feel it in the air. See the dust dance in the yellow light. Feel your hands dancing in the yellow light. Let it cover you. Let it embrace you and warm you. Breathe it in.

⤙ *Pause* ⤚

And now the light changes, and is green, light green at first, like Spring. Feel all the different colors of green in the light, from the palest green to the darkest, deepest green. Feel them all. Feel them on your skin. See them. See them on your hands; see all the greens on the walls of your cave. Feel them through your body. Taste them. Let your whole self be green with the light.

·≪ *Pause* ≫·

The light will change to blue now, to all the colors of blue. Feel them. Feel them on your skin, and see them. Dance in the blue light. Drink it in. Let the blue light remind you of water. Notice all the colors of blue on the walls of your cave. Notice all the colors of blue on your hands, and feel them all. Let your hands dance in the blue light. Let the blue light know everything about you. Let the beautiful blue light show you all of its colors.

·≪ *Pause* ≫·

The blue is getting darker now, and it's indigo. It's dark and rich and warm, and it has many shades to it. Feel it all over you; feel it within you. See it on your skin, feel it on your skin. See indigo on the walls of the cave—see how it deepens the shadows. Feel it inside and outside, and know that it is everywhere. It is soft and comfortable and strong. Relax with it, and let it swirl around you.

·≪ *Pause* ≫·

And let the indigo light turn to violet now. The sunlight in your cave is violet now, all the colors of violet. Let them dance with your hands, these violet colors. Feel how soft they are. Feel how the violet colors trust you, and feel how you trust them. See the violets on the walls of the cave, and see them on your hands. See the violet light, and let it see you, inside and out. Breathe it, taste it, let it come in and out of you like breath.

·≪ *Pause* ≫·

Now let the light be sunny gold again, touching you and touching the walls of your cave. Let the dust dance in it again, just for you.

Know that you have received a precious gift. Know that these colors are yours now, for ever and ever. These colors are yours to see and feel whenever you want them.

Remember how strong the colors are, and remember that you can use their strength, for they are yours now. They have been given to you in this very special cave, this cave that is yours alone. This experience is yours, all yours, and it is yours now and forever, whenever you need it. You have all the colors within you now, and they are safe with you, and you are safe with them. This secret cave is yours forever, too.

⋇ *Short Pause* ⋇

Look up now, through the crack in the top of the cave, and see that the sunlight has become moonlight, silvery and gentle. Feel it touch you softly, like a purring kitten. Feel it on your hands and face. Touch it. Hold it in your hands. Feel the Moon and the stars glitter in this silvery light. Feel the cool, tingling touch of this light inside you. Breathe it in. It is yours.

You can see the Moon and the stars through the roof of your cave. You can feel the cool, safe darkness and the sparkling of life all around you. You can feel the mysteries, you can touch them. You can breathe them and see them. You do not need to speak, for the Moon and the stars, and the light of evening and midnight, are deep within you now.

⋇ *Pause* ⋇

Lie down on the floor of your cave and enjoy this for as long as you like. Feel the moonlight, feel how gently it touches you. Notice how safe and comfortable you feel with the moonlight beside you. Hear the sounds of the night: the birds, the clouds, the darkness. Close your eyes and enjoy this for a little while.

⋇ *Pause* ⋇

Open your eyes now, and see the cave in sunlight again. Feel the floor of the cave beneath you, and slowly, slowly, get up—and you are standing again in the shaft of sunlight. This is magical light, it is all the light there is. It is the light of the Sun and the Moon and the stars; it is the light of life, and it is yours. It is strong light, and now its strength is yours. It will be yours forever, just like this cave. Like this cave, like the light, *you* are magical, and you always will be. The magic of the cave and the magic of the light live within you now.

You will take the magic with you when you leave your cave. You are leaving now, but you are not sad to go, for the magic is with you. You can come back here whenever you want to. It is your cave, and your magic.

You come back to the forest clearing now. The magic is still with you, and always will be. As you move back into the forest clearing—as quickly or as slowly as you want to—remember that the magic of the cave is with you. Remember that the magic and the cave and the light are yours to keep, forever.

You are back in the forest clearing now, and it is quiet but for the wind and the birds and the squirrels. Hear them. Listen for their songs and their footsteps. Lie down on the forest floor, and feel the strong Earth beneath you. Relax.

The grassy forest floor is safe and strong, and it will hold you. The Earth is your Mother, and She will hold you safely. You are safe and relaxed and comfortable here. Slowly, slowly, the clearing becomes the room you were in when you started. Now you can feel the arms of your chair. Now you can feel your feet on the floor.

⤞ Short Pause ⤝

You are still safe, you are still relaxed. In a moment, you will open your eyes and be in your house, safe and secure with people you love, with people who love you. When you open your eyes to home, you will wait for just a moment before you get up. And in that moment, you will remember the forest, and you will remember the cave, and you will remember the colors and the lights. You will remember the magic, and you will remember that it is yours. You will remember and know that the magic is yours, within you, now and forever.

⊰ Short Pause ⊱

Now you will get up, and you will be completely back at home. And deep within you, when you are very still and pay attention, you will still feel all the colors, and all the magic. Blesséd be. I love you.

A meditation can take a child on a traditional journey, to a river bank, into a cave, through the clouds. Such a tape can take a child successfully through a test, to the solution of a problem with a friend, to a restoration of trust in personal judgment, or to a comfortable decision among confusing alternatives.

Making that tape, you'll have time to ground and center your concern for your child's health and happiness so you don't confuse it with your own. Otherwise, your energies can confuse the child and make life much more difficult! (Of course, you can and should modify it in some small ways to fit your own circumstances.) It's a good idea to listen to the tape when you're finished to be sure that the narration is not confusing or unclear—and it's perfectly alright for grown-ups to enjoy the meditation, too. We all need reminders about the magic within.

Usually we work magic at Esbats, but some of our Sabbat rituals can be magical. This one was composed before we were formally Wiccan, but it still pleases us.

The Rite of the Autumn Equinox (1984)

Participants arrange themselves in a rough circle around an elf-light (more about elf-lights later) or group of candles. Each participant has matches.

In unison: *We light these fires to our hopes for this season of harvest.*

Each person puts a match to light the elf-light together, or in turn lights a candle. Each shares a hope for the spiritual harvest.

One says: *As tame and wild crops are the harvest of the Earth....*

All say: *so our visions and hopes are humanity's harvest.*

One says: *Nature directs us to gather in that which we have cultivated in ourselves....*

All say: *to reap what we have sown in the species' heart.*

One says: *As the harvest of the Earth begins....*

All say: *let us set at our table a place for our kin whose bodies hunger.*

One says: *Let us share as well the harvest of our hearts....*

All say: *and lay upon our Altars that which we harvest of peace.*

One says: *We light these candles to the harvest of the human spirit....*

All say: *where hope and fear become reality in the twilight of the cycle.*

One says: *We consecrate to the light of our vision, the work of our hands that manifests in our hearts....*

All say: *that the work of our hands at harvest be the work of peace.*

One says: *The harvest of peace calls forth adobe (bricks) from hope....*

All say,   *and peace is our shelter when Winter comes.*

In unison: *We light these candles to the hopes of our hearts for the harvest of our hands. We consecrate these candles to our hopes for this season of harvest. In the name of the planet, we conclude in peace.*

The Rede and the Law

An ye harm none, do as ye will.
What you put into the Worlds returns to your life threefold.

In our magical work, we're guided by the (Wiccan) Rede and the (Threefold) Law. Introducing young children to magic, we must remember that their understanding of the ways we can harm others is different from ours. You must keep in mind that their interpretation of the Rede cannot be the same as ours.

It's very important not to wield the Rede and the Law as clubs. It's easy to guilt-trip children (including those disguised as adults), and it hurts to be guilt-tripped. Adults often enough misinterpret the Law as an authoritarian rule that's enforced by a supernatural Big Brother. Children too young to think symbolically tend to take it quite literally, and taken like that, it becomes superstitious.

Instead of quoting the Law and the Rede to children in the primary grades, we can show them how to consider other people's feelings. Then later, when they hear the Rede and the Law as we more traditionally express them, they'll already have experience of their meaning. "I wonder how it would feel to...?" we can ask. "Has something like this ever happened to you?" "What do you think would feel good if _____ happened?"

These questions can't be asked accusingly, of course—and children's answers don't need to be coached or judged. If we want our kids to be able to work magic when they come of age, then we have to raise them with the magic of the God/dess' unconditional love, and trust that by our example and Hers, they will learn well.

It is not easy to live by Wiccan standards when our society presents us with so many obstacles to creative cooperation. But following Wiccan principles is actually a sort of spell, not spoken but expressed in our lifestyle, and a way to overcome those obstacles. The mundane ways you show your children will be every bit as important to them when they grow up as the rituals and chants you teach them.

If those mundane ways are consistent with the spiritual laws and rules of magic that we follow, then our lives and our children's will be closer to the God/dess, and the world will be a better place.

Rite or Wrong?

We must have some concern, I think, about the materials we use. Canyondancer and I don't buy much new leather or fur, but we do rescue it from the thrift shop now and again, mostly for ritual use. We buy a very little of it at shops like the one where Faerie Moon and I find some material (a "fabrics by the pound" place); and we do not contribute to the market for "exotics" at all.

When we do buy leather or fur, it's usually for ritual (or sacred costume) use, and is blessed to liberate the spirit of the animal from which it came. We don't buy exotic leather or fur—cow and rabbit is our limit. No snake, no mink or jungle cat, and no scarce or endangered feathers, either. Except for an occasional little decorative bird at the craft shop, or some dyed turkey feathers, I rarely buy feathers at all. If I need some, I can gather pigeon or dove feathers almost anywhere. We sometimes find jay, woodpecker, "red bird" feathers in the yard and at camp.

If we want something more unusual than that, we go to the zoo and look beside the bird enclosures and beside the big animal habitats, where birds from the same region often live, too. I've had to be patient, but I've found everything from goose to guinea fowl feathers there, from partridge to peacock. (You may have to pay special attention to be sure these don't become cat toys when you bring them home.)

When we camp, I make it a point to look for bones, too. I've found quite a number of them, which now grace our backyard rockeries. Most of them come from cows, but from wild-ranging cows, not farm cows.

We have some skulls, too, from squirrels and other small furries we haven't identified. (Do check with your local department of fish and game to be sure you're not picking up any feathers or bones you're not supposed to.)

We consider these finds—always treated reverently—to be gifts from the Gods. There is always energy left in them, energy we can feel. We respect this, and ask the spirit of the animal (even when we're not sure what it is!) to help make our yard and the Circle in it a safe and sacred place. We sometimes use these bones and feathers (and leather and fur) in charms or to decorate pouches. We've strung bird vertebrae on our Cords of Life at Mabon, for instance.

Although these pieces are more impressive than things with which we're more familiar—shells, for example—it's good to remember that most of our materials were once alive. The paper this book is printed on used to be a tree; things lived in it and under it, too. The shells you may have on a necklace, in a fish tank, or in a charm, once protected a little water creature. Cotton is harvested from living plants. Some plants are abused by modern farming techniques, as many animals are. The glass or ceramic mug from which you sip your tea was a mountain 1 million years ago, or maybe it was the seabed.

We didn't include any consecration or blessing for such materials in the first edition of *Family Wicca*, but here, we'll share a thank-you blessing to say over the wild or once-wild materials you use in charms, costumes, in ritual, or on the Altar to represent the God/dess, or an Element.

Thank-You Blessing

Once you flew, or crawled, or walked,
or sprouted up from stem or stalk.
Then you died so life might live,
and so to you my [our] thanks I [we] give.
On my Altar, in my spell, I will honor you as well.
In my use and memory, you will ever blesséd be.

Wicca teaches us that all of life is interrelated. Many of us reject the idea that humanity is the most important species on the planet, and hold that we have no right to extinguish any other forms on our own behalf. (Not a whole species, anyhow; one on one can be a little different, and I feel no guilt when I slap a mosquito.) We take this to mean that, when we decide what materials to use in mundane life or magical, we have to be satisfied that our use of it doesn't contribute to or result in its disappearing from the world.

Your family may make different decisions than we do about such materials. That's fine! The important thing is that you do *make* a decision. You should be able to explain to your children—and to anyone else who asks—why, in thealogical terms, you think it is or is not okay to use certain materials in ritual or recreation.

Whether or not to hex or curse is another question that Wiccans face. It's one that every Witch and every family must answer, for the Threefold Law knows no exceptions, and no one can take the responsibility of a curse for someone else.

Once, when I was extremely angry—and we've already talked about this a little bit in another context—I asked the God to build a Gate in the offender's bones and "bring him face to face with the Guardians in his marrow." This is as close to hexing or cursing someone as I have ever come, and as close as I ever will come. As you work, so are you worked. If you are willing to face the Guardian(s) of the Gate, you may not be out of bounds to challenge someone else to that experience. But honesty—naked in your rites, remember—is as important in magic as the incense and the flame.

"You can't heal if you can't hex" is a maxim we've all heard more than once. Does that mean that sometimes it's okay to curse somebody? We don't think so, and here's why:

Years ago, I was in the Explorer's room, soothing him to sleep, when—from my perspective—the room exploded. A rock had been hurled through the window by would-be burglars, to see if anyone would be roused. Canyondancer checked on us first, so by the time he went outside, the would-be burglars were gone, making plans after concluding that someone was home. We took the Explorer into our bed and closed his door against wind (and kitty escapes) through the broken window. Mindless vandalism, we thought, and didn't worry.

We didn't sleep soundly, though, because the Explorer was an active sleeper, and it's hard to drift off with a child's foot in your ear! A couple of hours later, when the rock-throwers entered the house through the window they'd broken, we were awake and heard them opening the door from the Explorer's room. Canyondancer was on his feet immediately, thundering across the bed, making fearsome noises. The intruders, at least as startled as we were, fled rather clumsily, knocking furniture about in their mad dash for the front door. They got nothing but bruises from the big wooden chair they ran into, and a good scare!

My experience was of full adrenaline: I felt like a high-powered car in high gear with the pedal to the metal, and the brakes on. I was shaking, and I was fierce, ready to defend my "cub." (The Explorer was about 3 1/2 years old then, and slept through both the rock and the intrusion.) I realized that if the burglars had followed their rock through the window, they'd have been dead men, even though but for our wits and our body chemistry, we are an unarmed household. If either of us had gotten our hands on the intruders, they'd have been hospitalized at least, and we'd not have felt the tiniest bit of guilt. So what's the problem with cursing or hexing?

The problem is this: As individuals, our resources are limited. When we're suddenly confronted with danger (especially to our families), we may not be able to control the powerful hormonal responses that have evolved to keep human beings alive. Either Canyondancer or I might have had to kill an intruder with our bare hands to protect each other or our child.

But when we're doing magic, we are drawing on resources beyond the ordinary. When we do magic, we are between the Worlds, and the resources of all the Worlds are at our disposal. That means there are more options open to us, creative, healing options that may not be available when we're facing an immediate physical danger.

Just as a city has more resources than a single household, a state has more resources than a city, and a nation has more resources than a state, so do Witches have greater resources in magical work than we or anyone else have in ordinary situations. We think that having all the Worlds' magic available to us obligates us to use it as consistently with Her laws as we can.

Nor do I demand aught of sacrifice, She tells us. *Love unto all beings is My law*. She is generous in giving us the powers of Her magic; shall we slap Her in the face with it?

Magical Children

The late Mr. [Fred] Rogers, trying to help children cope with the tremendous guilt most of them accumulate, said there's no such thing as magic, and that wishing can't make a thing happen. He was half-right. With very young children (and some adults, apparently), it's important to distinguish between wishes and magic, between "magical thinking" and magic; between fairy-tale magic and that which is real.

For children of any age, a wish can vent emotional energy the same way a romp in the playground can vent physical energy; wishes also express needs and interests or concerns, and this is how we should understand them. The magic Witches do requires intellect and will that children do not possess. (No insult is intended to your child, who is no doubt precocious; human brains don't fully mature until we're about 25 years old, that's all.) Adults' magic involves symbolic thinking and delaying gratification, capacities that small children do not have.

The fledgling magic that children can do is the magic of belief and feeling; sometimes they can't tell the difference. (Some adults have difficulty distinguishing between feelings and acts of will, too.) Effortlessly, children see a castle where physically there stands an unmade bed. Because they're not wearing the culture's yoke of agreed-upon reality, children can sincerely *act as if* almost anything!

Children need to become comfortable with Wiccan images early on so that the magic they do as initiated Wiccans will be its strongest. If the castle s/he built and played in as a little boy or girl is reconstructed as a temple or an astral retreat, its power will be amplified by that patina.

Children who grow up surrounded by Wiccan images and metaphors will find them in all their surroundings when they grow up. Their parents will have taught them where to look for Witchcraft, just as a lioness teaches her cubs where to look for nourishment and water. These children will not feel the discomfort of conversion their parents may have endured. For such kids, full-fledged magic will come easily, because it will never have gone away.

Parents who do bring their children into Circle with them need to be prepared for some distractions, and to design spells that will work in spite of interruptions. Properly directed, though, even a child's energy can help to work real magic. Even when it's not practical to bring a young child into a Circle to work magic with Mom and Dad, her energy can be directed toward the magical goal at almost any other time.

"Let's pretend this doll is our friend Dawn, and lets sing a song to make her well again," works very nicely—providing you've got Dawn's (or her mom's) permission to do that healing magic. The Explorer has sent energy he raised in his tae kwon do class to a needy friend, releasing it toward its goal in every block and punch. "Let's put this [unlit or electric] candle beside your bed so you can light up your dreams with it," might help kids with bad dreams. (Most moms find that "Let me kiss it and make it better" works pretty darn well, too!)

By incorporating elements and techniques of real magic into a child's activity, the child's energy is directed helpfully; the child will be familiar with the tools and techniques later on, when s/he joins Mom and Dad (or another coven) in working. With young children, this integration should be carefully guided, and a child shouldn't be given any "ways" s/he's not free to work with in solitary play.

Explaining magic to a child who lives in a culture that diminishes magic to special effects and stage tricks can be difficult. At about the same time a child begins to grasp symbolic thinking, s/he is also developing the skills of logical reasoning, and cultural influences can make a child skeptical. (All the behind-the-scenes shows and DVD segments that break down the special effects of movie magic contribute to the idea that everything's just a trick. At the same time, increasingly realistic effects confuse us about reality: not long before I finished this revision, it was necessary to remind people that flushing goldfish down the toilet does not send them to freedom in the sea, no matter what happened in Disney's *Finding Nemo*.)

The transition from childhood to adolescence produces great energy, energy which our culture teaches us to invest in insecurity and self-doubt in an effort to control the power it represents. Directing energy is Witchcraft's specialty, and a skill that, once learned, is ever-useful, especially when things get rough.

One way to introduce children to Wiccan ritual and magic is through their own magical logic. A favorite "blankie" spread out on the floor or ground can be a child's first "Circle." (Fold under the edges of the blanket's corners if its square or rectangular shape bothers you; or fold them on top and let them mark the Quarters.) A favorite doll or stuffed toy can stand as a Goddess or God figure.

"Let's let Froofie be a wild animal and stand for the freedom of life in the forest," or "While Smiley Sally's on this blanket, she can be the Great Mommy of the whole world!" There's no reason why your child's collections of dolls, figures, or plush beasts can't make a Circle and work for Froofie's safe return from the washing machine, or for anything else that's important to your kid, either.

When the Explorer and his friends chose their "guys" from the toy box in the back room (an eclectic group, I might add, from different sets and with different accessories, yet all quite cooperative with each other), they each marked out territories within which their "guy" was invulnerable. Before they got into the action, they marked their boundaries and made the rules for crossing them clear. It's not far from this to defining the boundaries of a Circle and the rules for casting it, entering and leaving, and dismissing it.

As you watch your kids play, you'll see lots of opportunities to say, "When you do this, it's kind of like when we..." or, "When we do this, it's kind of like when you...." You may also be able to explain some Wiccan practices to your kids' friends with such analogies, if and when that's appropriate.

You've already "met" our good friend and initiate, Chandra Nelson, priestess of Hearth's Gate Coven, who shares an experience she had with her daughter: "Ivy's pet turtle died when she was four years old. We buried it in the backyard. After our memorial service I went back inside. I looked out my kitchen window to find that Ivy was watering the grave with the hose. I found this curious, so I went out to ask why. Ivy said that she knew that he would be reborn, and she know that if you water sunflowers they come back, so.... Of course this is flawed logic, and quite a lengthy conversation explaining how rebirth works followed."

Most of us experiment with skepticism (and sometimes it's healthy), and as they get older, your kids probably will, too. It's an approach to logic, and it's okay. You don't have to worry if your kid wants her magic to stand to reason—because magic does. So much magic is obviously compatible with what we know of natural law that we can pretty easily trust that all of it is.

One way of making this clear to your kids is in terms of examples from your own family life. "If you tell me that you want a chocolate cake for your birthday, you know that telling me is enough, right? You don't have to be there when I buy the mix or bake it to know it will be chocolate, do you? And you can trust that the cake is chocolate even if it has vanilla frosting, can't you? Just so, when we're working magic, we're telling the God/dess what we need, and we know that's enough. We don't have to understand exactly how She works, and we don't have to worry if it looks different than we thought it would—has a different flavored frosting—either."

You'll know what your kids wonder and worry about, and what metaphors and examples they'll understand. If you don't react defensively, if you accept their wary curiosity and work with it instead of against it, you'll be able to address their concerns effectively. When your son or daughter says, "Aw, come on, how can that work?" don't be afraid to answer in terms of experience.

Can't most of us tell when friends are angry or happy or scared, even if the friend says nothing or denies it? And don't our friends' moods affect us? Have your children ever been worried about something, or totally immersed in sadness or fear, and then suddenly, when new information becomes available or somebody understands after all, been completely relieved? Has a good friend ever done just the right thing, even when your child didn't even know what s/he wanted that friend to do? Has something that interests your child ever, a day or so later, been all over the television and the papers, or brought up by teachers and friends, out of the blue?

Right there, you have the basic mechanics of magic. It is possible—and your children will know this from their own experience if you point it out to them—to influence and be influenced by other people and the world *by and through energy*.

Wicca is a religion of experience, and you can show your children how to interpret their experience in Wiccan terms (as well as in scientific and psychological terms). And that little "oh!" that you hear from them or see in their eyes or in their smiles of understanding? That's magic too.

Some Simple Rituals and Magics

The spiral is an ancient symbol of the process of life, and holds great power. It is an image that speaks volumes and transcends cultural distinctions. When you use it in a spell, you call upon 10s of thousands of years of human energy and add it to your own. Here are some spiral spells that you and your children can use in your work.

The Salt Spiral

You will need a plain white sheet of paper (or a white napkin, or an undecorated paper plate), a crayon in a color suitable to your purpose, and salt. Salt is a symbol of the Earth's strength and purity. Before you cast this spell, bless the salt. Draw a pentagram over it (right in the box is fine) and say, "Blesséd be, you Creature of Earth. Banish all fear from this place and bless my work with your strength."

Kyle (left) and Ivy (right) demonstrate making salt pictures of something they want to bring into their lives. They're working on a patch of dirt so they can dump the salt onto it when they're done, rather than tossing it into the air.

With the crayon, draw a dot or symbol in the center of the paper. This represents the work you want to do, your goal. Focus your mind on this goal. Starting at the outer edge of the paper, draw an in-winding spiral with the Salt, finishing with a small mound to cover the dot in the center. Think or talk about your goal as you draw the spiral.

When you have put your energy into the spiral of Salt, press both your thumbs into the mound of Salt in the middle, to seal your work. Sealing the spell this way binds your energy to the spell, and allows it to keep receiving energy from the world. After you have sealed the spell, fold the paper so that all the Salt comes to the center.

If you spill any, pick it up with your moistened finger, and then lick your finger to put the Salt on your tongue and make the spell a part of you. Now, either bury the folded paper in your yard, or put it in a pouch and hang it somewhere safe. Every time you walk near it or see it, you'll recharge it and keep it working. When the goal has been achieved, you may burn the paper with some words of thanks.

The Yarn Spiral

For this work you'll need a large open space—a big, grassy yard or park would be great—and a skein of yarn in a color suitable to your purpose. Let your child choose the color, for children make very strong associations, and insisting on an orthodox correspondence may divert their energy. Choose a word or a short phrase (as in a mantra) to represent the spell's goal.

Your child should hold the pulling end of the yarn (the one from the inside, not the outer one) to his/her solar plexus, where his/her ribs meet just below the middle of his/her chest. You'll need to hold the skein and make sure it doesn't get hung up and interrupt the working. You can let small knots or tangles go by; just keep the yarn feeding until the spell is done.

Your child should begin turning in a circle, slowly at first, and changing the word or phrase that represents his/her goal. Gradually, s/he'll spin

On the left, mom Brandyn supervises son Reece and friend's daughter Brylelyn as they try out a Yarn Spiral. In the right-hand photo, mother and daughter, Chandra and Ivy, demonstrate that winding the yarn too tight can be a problem!

faster and faster, getting wrapped in the yarn, and probably dizzy. S/he may stagger or even fall down. If that happens, shout the word or phrase as the child falls. If s/he doesn't fall, s/he should keep going till the yarn's used up, and then fall down on purpose, shouting the word or phrase.

Without unwinding the yarn (make nine knots and break the strand between the last knot and the skein if there's any left over), slide this enormous spiral off your child. This spiral has been wound toward the outside, sending its energy toward the goal. The yarn can be kept as a charm, knotted to intensify the spell, or burned (outside, please—it won't smell pleasant, and you might like to burn some incense at the same time) to seal it forever, and send additional energy through Fire and Air.

Story Spells

Children love to tell stories. You can help your child cast a story spell with scissors and—yes—construction paper! Cut out shapes to represent the characters in the story, which are the elements of the spell. Story spells can be used in all sorts of ways: to solve problems, to prepare for challenging events, to clarify feelings. Here's an example of a story spell used for healing.

If you want to help someone get well, and you have their permission to help them heal, you might cut out the shapes of a bed, the patient, and another figure to represent your child. Let your child choose the color(s) of the paper, and if s/he's old enough, design and cut the figures, too.

Using the cut-out figures, enact the healing. Let your child act it out, dancing the figures around on a table or on the floor, and telling a story of recovery. If your child is working on a self-healing, the third cut-out might represent the Goddess or the God or another comforting figure.

When the story has been told (maybe several times), your child can make a symbol on each figure—initials or a healing sign—and put all the figures in an envelope with the patient's figure on top of the others. Then your child can mail the envelope to the friend the spell is meant to help, or put it under the friend's pillow during a visit. If the envelope stays at a safe place in your house, then when the situation is resolved, your child can (with your supervision) burn the envelope with some words of thanks.

This is a form of sympathetic magic. Our ancestors left their figures on cave walls. If your child would prefer to draw a story spell, great. Use chalk on the sidewalk or patio, or paper taped to the wall. Older children may want to write their stories down, and maybe even read them aloud to an appropriate audience—to the person they're meant to heal, or to someone who can influence the outcome of the situation the spell addresses. (For more about story spells, please read *Raising Witches*, wherein this book is quoted and there's a longer explanation and more examples.)

I did some story magic when I was young, before I knew what it was. I wrote about marrying a professor, and having a son—which is exactly what I did when I grew up. And when a high-school friend and I wrote completely fantastic stories that combined elements of the First World War (then being played out in *Peanuts* comic strips) with our concerns about Vietnam, we were astonished to find elements of those stories appearing in the newspaper! One of our characters was the Red Baron; we had him reappearing in Vietnam with a pet boa constrictor, of all things. About a week after we wrote that, there was a photo in the (Portland) *Oregonian* of a young medic whose nickname was the Red Baron, and who had a pet boa! This is why I recommend story spells with such confidence.

No magic can contravene natural law, but natural law works through energy, and we can influence energy. When energy is in motion, when "things are happening," we sometimes want to give that energy a nudge in one direction or another. Story spells are one kind of nudge; the following candle magic is another.

Tipping the Scales

You will need two candles, one to represent the way things seem to be going, and one to represent the way you'd like them to go. Make these two candles as different in color as you can. It's up to you whether to use votives, tapers, pillars, or more decorative candles; some shops carry candles in a variety of shapes, and there's a wide selection of theme-shaped candles for birthday cakes, so maybe you can find one that will pretty much exactly represent the work you mean to do.

Set up the "seems to be" candle and light it while you think about the situation you'd like to influence. As you watch the flame, think or talk about the way you'd like to change what seems to be happening. When you have a clear picture of the change you'd like to affect, pick up the "like to be" candle and hold it in both hands.

Concentrate for a few moments on the change you'd like to see. When that image is very strong, light the "like to be" candle from the "seems to be" candle, and *immediately* extinguish the "seems to be" candle with your moistened thumb and forefinger. (Obviously, this spell is not for very young children to work. If your child is old enough to light candles like this but disinclined to put one out this way, s/he can spit into a snuffer and use that. The point is to use some physical part of yourself in extinguishing the "seems to be" candle.)

If possible, let the "like to be" candle burn down. If you can't do that, then let it burn one minute for every year of your child's age, and then extinguish it the same way you put out the "seems to be" candle. Then burn the "like to be" candle the same number of minutes every day until it's gone, even if things work out the way you want them to before the candle has burned all the way down.

Young children can stomp their feet rhythmically and chant to raise energy. They can release that energy toward a goal by jumping onto a picture they've drawn of the goal. They can draw pictures in dirt or sand and dance the Witches' Rune; you can chant and drum while your child dances.

With their fingers they can stir a bowl of Salt, making signs that represent what they want to happen (Mickey Mouse ears in the Salt when they want to go to Disneyland, for instance), and then fling the charged Salt into the air. All eyes should be tightly closed when the Salt is flung (outside), partly to symbolize trust that the Mother will use the energy in the service of life and your goal, and partly to protect all eyes from the flying salt, which can burn painfully.

You will think of other ways to use traditional Wiccan symbols and tools (and to modify the spells in this book and others, adapting them to your kids' ages and needs) to introduce your children to magic; and your children will have some ideas, too.

There are, of course, two parts to working any magic: the *magic* and the *working*. A child's work is different from an adult's, but just as important. What we all need to remember is that magic is alive through us, through our lives, and the more energy we put into our magic and into our lives, the better both our lives and our magic will be.

Chapter Five

Answering the Hard Questions

Every parent, and most friends, eventually has to answer hard questions for children and other people. Why did someone I love do such a terrible thing? Why did such a terrible thing happen to someone I love? Why am I alive? What's all this stuff about sex, anyway? Why do people think we're Satanists? Was that my fault? What happens when I die?

We think it's terribly important to answer these questions in Wiccan terms. Sometimes we have to rephrase the question before we can answer it. You can't answer a question such as, "Why does one plus one equal three?" because one plus one *doesn't* equal three. You can't answer a question such as, "Why does God want me to suffer?" either.

Here are some of our questions and answers—and remember, questions that have been asked for thousands of years take more than 30 seconds to answer! (We look at some of these questions in *Raising Witches* and *In the Service of Life*, too, so to explore these questions in slightly different contexts, please read those books. They both complement this one nicely.)

Why Am I Alive?

Well, Mommy and Daddy love each other very much, and when a man and a woman love each other very much....If that (or the Mommy and Mum or Papa and Daddy variant) isn't the answer your kid is looking for, try this: because Life is the nature of the universe.

There are questions to which the answer really is "because that's the way it is." Stephen Hawking, in *A Brief History of Time*, says that questions about what was before the Big Bang are not only impossible to answer but irrelevant, because the Bang was a singularity: something that, when it happens, changes things so much that afterwards is utterly, indescribably, incomparably different than anything that was before. We accept this. Once the Goddess saw herself in the mirror, as Starhawk's creation story puts it, once her joy exploded, nothing was the same. The Big Bang was material, the Goddess' creation of consciousness its spiritual aspect. And it is the nature of each that they are metaphors for each other.

They are inseparable and yet distinguishable, and inevitable. We are alive because we evolved (and there were atoms from which we could evolve because there was a Bang—because the Goddess is and existence is Her nature).

Okay, But What Are We Supposed to Do About It?

Ah, well, that one's a little easier. We're supposed to do as we will, and we harm none. We're supposed to love all beings. We're supposed to be aware (of our needs, for instance, so that whenever we have any, we can gather in some sacred place).

Other religions assert that humanity's purpose is to serve and glorify a god. Generally they are quite specific about which god and how to serve and glorify. The Goddess calls all acts of love and pleasure Her rituals, so that the solitary enjoyment of a summer's afternoon is as worshipful as a formal Circle; but worship is only one way Wiccans fulfill life's purpose.

126

Being a religion of experience rather than dogma, Wicca holds that the purpose of life is—life. So when the Explorer wanted to know why he was alive, we told him that he's alive to experience as much as he can. To love, to create, to run in the wind, to cry, to hope, to dream. To chill your toes in mountain streams, we told him; to watch the ants on the sidewalk, to ask how to spell p-l-a-t-y-p-u-s, to drift into oneness with the atmosphere halfway up the mountain; to see the in the darkness of the cave, to hold another hand in a Circle under the moon, to keep his Maypole ribbon tight as we dance; to pet the cat.

And when he wanted to know if that was all, we'd ask him what else he imagines there might be, and you know what? He'd smile in that sudden secret understanding that is, ultimately, the only reason any of us need to be alive.

Why Do Bad Things Happen? Am I Bad?

No! "Bad" things happen for a number of reasons. Sometimes, they are the natural consequences of hasty, uninformed, or misinformed choices. Sometimes, they're the result of someone's ignorance, fear, or chemical incompleteness. Some things are beyond human control. A distinction we use is between *something we did wrong* and *something that happened to us*.

We don't talk about fault or blame—we talk about responsibility. Fault and blame imply guilt, and guilt keeps us powerless; responsibility implies authority and the power to correct and learn from our mistakes. That power is God/desses' gift to all of us; we don't presume to deny it to anyone.

Sometimes a thing that seems bad when it happens turns out to be the proverbial blessing in disguise. The God/dess, as we all know, works in mysterious ways. More practically than that, though, some of the things we call bad could be called something else: an inconvenience, a challenge, an opportunity, a change in plans (and maybe all of the above).

Although it can be difficult to find purpose and inspiration in everything that happens, it is a worthwhile undertaking. (When I sat down to revise this book, I opened the disk with the original version on it, and found the folder empty. So instead of editing, I'm retyping. And I'm trusting that this is wonderful, rather than just annoying.) When things proceed according to plan, it's easy to take things for granted. When our expectations are challenged by random occurrences—a burglar's strike, an inexplicable stroke—you may be laid low. While you are sprawled upon the ground, you have an opportunity to explore its depths and strengths—and your own depths and strengths as well. You don't have to just bite the dust or eat dirt; you can choose to be nourished. Changing your perception of something that's happened sometimes gets you laughed at, but it is at the heart of magic. Another way of appreciating the value of changed perspective is sociopolitical: are men who have long hair and beards, for instance, dang-blasted sissy commie-pinko bums, or are they fully masculine, free, and natural?

At the Explorer's tae kwon do class years ago, I overheard a conversation between two dads that illustrated this point well. Putting his pocket Bible down for a moment, one asked the other if he'd let his son grow long hair. The second father answered that he might, as long as it wasn't too long.

"To his shoulders?" the first dad asked.

"Oh, no!" the second dad exclaimed. "I think boys should look like boys."

Sitting next to them, it was all I could do not to say that yeah, my favorite picture of their Jesus has always been the one with his hair in a crew cut.

Was it a curse that Canyondancer was unable to find a job teaching political science at a liberal arts university, or the gateway to his destiny? If you'd asked us when we first found out that his position at a small school in Missouri wasn't tenure-track after all, when we had a mountain of debts and the Explorer was barely a year old, when we had to wire my parents for money to pay the movers who'd raised their price at the last minute, we might have called it a bad thing. But now we call it the first step on the path to the life we live now, and we wouldn't trade it for all the honest movers in Missouri or all the tenured positions in academia.

Is There No Divine Punishment for Evildoing?

No, we don't believe there is—only the healing, only the learning, only the wholeness. "But it seems so unfair!" Does it? Love unto all beings is Her law. One of my favorite chants is *Where there's fear, there can be no love/where there's love, there can be no fear.* Punishment is revenge, revenge is fear, and fear precludes love.

Self-realization is love, and in the Summerland, we realize ourselves and our Self. And on Earth, the natural consequences of unloving behavior are severe—the solitary confinement to which we are sentenced by so many social norms is punishment enough. This does not mean that unacceptable behavior has to be tolerated. It only means that we will protect ourselves from it most effectively if we act from love rather than succumbing to the same fear that motivates a wrongdoer. We need to draw upon the resources that cooperation gives us, rather than accepting the isolation wrongdoers feel and try to impose on everyone else.

I was asked about people "getting away with" doing harm to others at a workshop I was giving a couple of days after my wedding rings had been stolen. I admitted to mentioning the theft to a couple of pretty scary goddesses, but said equally truthfully that by then, 36 hours later, my sincere intent was that the love in those rings would have a positive effect in the lives of the people they touch from now on. My point was that any of us who feel like victims of harm need to remember that we have the power—and the attendant responsibility—to spin the energy that harm raises in us, and turn it to constructive work in the world.

Why Did Someone I Love Do [Such] a Bad Thing?

Fear, most likely. Of course, there are people whose brains are chemically incomplete: "glitchy," we call it, but fear can be just as crippling as an organic chemical imbalance. Whether a bad thing is done "by choice" or without control, there's fear behind it. Ironically, the most heinous offenses are usually committed out of the fear of being unloved.

And How Should We Respond to People Who Do Bad Things?

First, we must restrain them. We must do so from an understanding of their pain—yes, their pain. Love unto all beings cannot manifest if we don't acknowledge others' needs as equally as important as our own. Then we must provide for them an environment in which their fear is diminished. Otherwise, we only nurture the perversion of nature that moved them to act wrongly. Above all, we must not give in to our own fears.

Whether we're talking about violence on the streets or our children's smart-mouthing, loss of control is scary. Our ancestors lived in peace for 10s of thousands of years in an environment over which they had much less control than we exercise today; how is it that our society is so impotent? We think it has a lot to do with unrealistic expectations. Witches do not appreciate the fundamentalist [Christian] expectation, for instance, that everyone on the planet should accept Jesus as their personal savior. But white America cannot seem to understand that other cultures might not appreciate an expectation that they will adopt WASP standards of beauty, of social structure, of personal worth.

If we shared the God/dess' unconditional love with each other—Her sheer joy and Her courage, Her daring, Her humor, Her sense of adventure—we could appreciate our differences, and not hide from them or deny them or condemn them. With our fear of each other gone, we would not need to interact defensively. I sometimes talk about fields of wild flowers, pointing out the cultural consensus that variety in that context is good. Then I wonder aloud why, when we can appreciate the natural variety of hundreds of kinds of flowers, we get so uptight about the natural variety of the rest of life, including ourselves.

The transformation of a society as rewarding of aggression as ours is, of institutions as bureaucratically defended as ours are, is not something that can be achieved overnight. But it is something that can be achieved, if we do not cloud our vision with fear. The transformation of a bully into a friend is not easy, but it is, as boomers are wont to say, "doable." The force that is life in all its complexity is not incapable of such a thing, and we are that force, for that is God/dess.

What About This Sex Business, Anyway?

The only time sex is bad is when it is a business. No, I have to qualify that: obviously, rape in any of its forms is not a good thing either. Anything people do is bad when it's exploitive. (This includes child molestation and child porn, even though both of these enterprises deal more with control than sex.) There's nothing intrinsically bad about sex, though, and nobody's body isn't beautiful.

Overhearing preadolescent conversations, it's painfully obvious that a lot of children know nothing about the urges they're beginning to feel. They know some "dirty words," and these days, they know some "dirty moves," but they're abysmally ignorant about their own anatomies and what changes to expect—"You can get pregnant from doorknobs and toilets," somebody whispers; "So-and-So's got hair," somebody else will exclaim, "so he has to use deodorant."

The presumption that nothing about our bodies is good, or at least not good enough, comes partly from religious teachings that the physical world belongs to the devil and partly from the modern culture's narrow definitions of beauty and success. The sense of unworthiness is all-pervasive.

131

Our bodies are "nasty," as kids sometimes put it; our children may leave that notion behind, but some of their friends never will.

From this ignorance and a premise that bodies are fundamentally "icky" (while their sense of worth is tied to their bodies, and those reduced to commodities), how can they appreciate any experiences their bodies give them? Instructed that their bodies belong to the devil and are displeasing to their god—an instruction reinforced by beatings and mockery that are taken for granted in more families than you'd like to think—how can they respect anyone else's body?

How will they trust their instincts if their instincts are vilified and repressed? How will they value their lives? The sad truth is that many of them won't—and the sadder truth is that when they grow up (if they grow up), they'll be part of a whole society that does not love its body, politic or physical. This horrific attitude contributes to the problem of drug addiction, crime, homelessness, and other cultural corruption. (It also contributes to the awful abuse of children that is not dealt with because our culture's either in denial about it, or ineffectually paranoid.)

Much of the fear most people feel, physically, socially, economically, comes from their understanding of their bodies—and by extension, the rest of themselves—as bad, unworthy. The conflict that patriarchal monotheism has deliberately constructed between our hormones and our higher selves is not natural; accepting it as such makes us schizophrenic.

We believe that the Goddess gave us both sides of our brains—and a connecting organ—so that we can live in wholeness. Patriarchal faiths have cut the connection, much as mental patients used to be lobotomized (some still are) so they'd be easier to control.

It was said that with the AIDS epidemic, the sexual revolution was over. We say it has not yet begun: what looked like revolution at first turned out to be just getting dizzy. Promiscuity is not freedom, it's just slavery to a different master; the Goddess both blesses and charges us with freedom from slavery. Notches on the shaft aren't the signature of joy. Mindlessness is neither love nor pleasure.

The fear that still guides our society's sexual quest only makes us aggressive: fear makes us defensive, and we're told that the best defense is a good offense. There is no such thing as a good offense, though, and neither an erect penis nor an open vulva (or Justice's naked breast) has to be offensive. Rather, they should be sacred, for they are life itself. *That's* what about all this sex business.

The joy can be restored, of this we are sure. Whether or not passionate rhetoric is your family's style, there are other ways of communicating healthy sexual attitudes. If your focus is on respect for privacy, which goes beyond the toilet, rather than on concealment of body parts, then skyclad needn't ever feel naughty. If you use "real names" for your anatomies—"penis," not "wee," and "vagina," not "down there"— then more subtle nonclinical metaphors will not be meaningless or uncomfortable.

We have to remember that before we come through puberty, we don't appreciate sex. We can understand it intellectually—technically—once we're age 7 or so, but until we're pubescent, we don't get behind it emotionally. Our kids may well roll their eyes and wrinkle their noses and go, "Eeeewww, girls!" or "Eeeewww, boys!" It doesn't mean they'll never have a merry May Day.

Most parents have been interrupted at lovemaking by their children. The popular culture laughs at this situation, making rather crude jokes to mask discomfort. The awkwardness and fear that witnessing the sex act will warp our kids comes from guilt, imposed by patriarchal custom. From our perspective, all acts of love and pleasure are Her rituals, but this is far from a social standard. Love expressed through sex is still crude, and our bathroom-joke attitude has been exaggerated and imposed on the culture to the extent that in the summer of 2003, American TV executives were horrified at the idea that a couple making love would send a friend for a condom; but shows about murder and mayhem (or power-over expressed through sex), and news that crooked executives can steal millions from trusting investors, are fine commercial draws. Responsible sex is bad, violence (physical and economic) is okay. Gosh.

When the Explorer, Canyondancer, and I hugged each other, as we often did when the boy was small, we called it a "together hug." When the Explorer was young and came into our room one night when we were making love, we paused to see what he would say or do. He approached us with a sleepy smile and outstretched arms and said, "Can I have some of that together hug?"

Of course he could! We each reached out an arm, and the three of us embraced; he went back to bed, and we went back to our midnight motion. I think the same thing happened a few more times when he was little, and he shows no signs of being warped. What he does show signs of is trusting, and knowing that love can be everywhere. Whether, back then, he was ever aware that we were having sex, I don't know. He was aware that people do; he knew early on where babies come from because he'd seen the pictures of his own birth, and had attended two other home-births.

He also learned that sex is only part of love, and only one of the body's many wonderful capacities. Unlike some of his friends (and some of ours, and some of yours, too, no doubt), he understands that not all hugs between men and women are sexual. In other words, because he was never taught that anything about his body is taboo, nothing is. Oh, he learned early that we all need privacy, for things like going to the bathroom. And he knew before he went to school that there are some pleasures of the body we don't share with other people, or only with very special other people, and he knew why.

It's because some pleasures and parts of our bodies and souls are so special that we want to share them only with people who are equally special, and special in certain ways. One picks one's quest-companions very carefully, after all, not on the spur of the moment or on the basis of one or two tastes in common.

We need to respect our children's feelings so they can respect their feelings, and feel comfortable with them all their lives. Otherwise, we risk teaching our children to acknowledge only certain feelings, skewing their perception and disabling them emotionally. Sex is a matter of life and death in more ways than one; that's why it's sacred to us. And that's why it's important—a moral obligation, really—to address it as families. Like death, sex is an agent of transformation, a holy mystery.

Our culture tries to take initiation into that mystery for granted (or for profit). We've become conditioned to instant gratification. From television, for instance, we learn that problems should be solved in half an hour, or an hour, and that a lot of the work done to solve them is done invisibly, during the commercials. (This is an example of "magical" or "fairy-tale" thinking.) Consequently, the significance of sex and other important aspects of our lives has been distorted, its real meaning reduced to entertainment, hidden in obsession, and subjugated to commercialism.

We've been robbed of our natural joy, forced to be defensive and insensitive. On top of that, we're overwhelmed by the violence and unresolved anger and grief for our unrealized loss. As Wiccans, we believe it is within our power to restore the natural balances. But we must also be willing to undertake the initiatory task of both-brain awareness to restore the sanctity of our sexuality. (All of this is about heterosexuality, homosexuality, and autosexuality; all that's normal and fine. Anything that involves real threats, exploitation, and/or fear...isn't.)

Why Do Some People Think We're Satanists?

A long time ago, when the Christian armies were expanding their empires, they found native Pagan populations uncooperative. Just as invaders do now, they called the natives subhuman, and uncivilized.

Misinterpreting indigenous customs they did not understand, the conquerors tried to make sense of unfamiliar religions using standards that did not legitimately apply. The sense they made was that it was okay to slaughter these people, and that they were justified in burning their temples and enslaving their children.

They also concluded that it was alright to excoriate their faiths and demean their gods, and ridicule and vilify their relationship with each other and the world; even alright to invent new interpretations of their own (Christian) faith so that conquered Pagans' gods could be more easily demonized.

Too hard to explain? Try an analogy of playground or office politics. Call the "enemy" names, deliberately misinterpret questions and conversations, even lie. Arrange mistakes that will seem to be the "enemy's" fault. Recruit allies with false accusations and empty promises. It's a dire story, old and new at the same time.

What historical details our children and the rest of our families are ready to hear is different for each of us, but the situation can be made plain to anyone of (almost) any age. It's not Christian-bashing to tell this truth; Europe's Pagans did not ask to be enslaved and burned—nor did the Christians we know today forge the chains or light the fires. In fact, there are more and more Christians who know enough about Wicca to respect the faith, and who accept Wiccan clergy as their peers; we are pleased to have the impression that the number of such Christian ministers is growing.

There are still some people who walk around with lighters and kindling in their pockets. Their credibility is diminishing as more and more people understand more clearly that Wicca is a life-affirming faith, and that Satanism is a Christian heresy.

Death

Death is one of popular culture's last taboos. Most of us don't want to face it except in contexts so protected that we are not really touched.

Sad or gory movies (and 2003's new-low TV series, *Scare Tactics*, along with a few others that feature dreadful practical jokes meant to frighten and/or humiliate) let us project our fear and guilt. Even when death is almost dripping into our laps from the big and little screens, we don't have to face it.

In real life, death is more than a special effect, and as our society thrashes about in waste, destruction, hypocrisy, cynicism, war, deceit, and hopelessness, we, more and more often, have to face it. Because death and loss are a part of everyone's life, and because we are so detached by social customs, we think it's very important for Wiccan families to be aware of Witchcraft's perspectives. Otherwise, we'll be unprepared and afraid—untrusting and loveless—when we get to the Gates, and that's a fate truly worse than death.

Since the first edition of *Family Wicca* came out, I've written a book that looks at death more closely. *In the Service of Life: a Wiccan Perspective on Death*, was published by Kensington Books in 2003. Death will always be sad; it doesn't have to be scary. I do recommend that you and your family explore the subject in greater depth, together, with the help of *In the Service of Life*; here, as we did in the first edition, we're going to touch on the subject only briefly.

When the young son of a man I know was very seriously injured in an accident, I was called to the hospital to minister to the parent. He is not a Wiccan, but his own minister was out of town, and his estranged family lived in distant states. He knew a little about Witchcraft from some of our conversations, and his secret hope was that I could wave my magic wand and change medical reality, which was grim.

What I could do for him, and what proved to offer more comfort than the fear and guilt that were the foundations of his early religious training, was hold him and let him cry, and help him face the very real possibility of his not-yet-10-year-old son's death. Members of his church rallied in the waiting room, but no one was comfortable with his tears, and no one would say the "d-word."

Sometimes there is no sense to be made of things. This is difficult to accept, and especially in the absence of a strong conviction that the world is by nature "friendly," a temptation to lay blame can be strong. But my friend was not a bad parent to have a son who was walking one day in the wrong place at the wrong time; no god was punishing the boy for breaking dad's rules about staying home. No one was at fault. It was a horrible accident. (I am pleased to be able to report now that the boy survived, with some, but very minimal, brain damage, and is now a successful grown-up. His dad enjoys who Pete is, and no longer guilt-trips himself about who Pete might have been had the accident not changed their lives.)

Serious accidents, such as chemical imbalances in our brains, or birth defects, are glitches in the natural order, not demonstrations of the fundamental hostility of life. They do not happen for the reasons we misunderstand karma to provide. We give them reason, we choose to let these events change our lives, and we make the deaths we mourn meaningful, not in vain. These accidents do not happen deliberately to punish us because we have in our sinfulness thrown life out of balance. Rather, when these accidents divert life's creativity, it is within our natural power to restore the balance by our responses to physical, emotional, and social trauma.

This restoration of senseless death or loss to the service of life cannot be accomplished from feelings of fear or guilt, but the restoration we make becomes, through our own power and by our own choice, the reason for the loss. It's not cause-and-effect; the loss hasn't any inherent reason, but *we* do.

And our restorative energy is generated by love and trust, the same love and trust in which Wiccans reenter the Circle. Grief need not ever be denied, but fear and guilt need not always attend it. When dogmatically imposed fear and guilt do attend grief, it cannot regenerate or heal as it is biochemically and spiritually meant to do.

"Nor do I demand aught of sacrifice, for behold, I am the Mother of all things, and My love is poured forth across the lands," the Goddess tells us in one version of the *Charge*. A death in the family can feel like sacrifice, but the Goddess is true to Her word. Death is not a sacrifice, for you need not give up anything to it: life's form's change, but life does not end.

A life's influence is not diminished by its transformation, either. Knowing that the spirit is eternal, you can trust that love—a function of spirit—is eternal, too. Indeed, beyond death, freed from the limitations of a physical body, love's expressions can be even greater. "On Earth, I give knowledge of the Spirit Eternal," the Goddess promises, "and beyond death, I give peace, and freedom, and reunion with those who have gone before."

Though letting go of a dying loved one or accepting other drastic changes is painful, you know you are not turning your belovéd or yourself out into some trackless wilderness. No, you are releasing that spirit to the care of our Mother—who better to care for those you love? Through the Mother we are all reborn; the very life you are living right now is beyond death.

What Happens When I Die?

People who have returned from death tell us that they leave their bodies to survey the scene. Despite the surprise they may feel, they are usually calm, and can often remember conversations held over their bodies. After spending some time in a corner of the ceiling, they're distracted and drawn into a long tunnel, which is sometimes noisy and alarming, but which usually becomes a light that is more than a light, a sort of living incandescence.

Virginia Woolf associated incandescence with genius, suggesting that genius cannot find expression through a mind that has not burned away all bitterness, fear, and other such distractions. The Goddess promises freedom beyond death; freedom from those very impediments to our natural genius for life. She (the Goddess, not Virginia Woolf) is, after all, that which is attained at the end of all desire, "desire" meaning the basic mortal needs and senses by which we're aware of being separate from the Whole.

As people die, sometimes the living light alone greets them; sometimes they perceive it as a welcoming figure. There is never any fear once a person has seen the light. Wicca calls the experience of this serene light, this peace, the Summerland. Canyondancer and I told our son about the tunnel, and explained to him that the light's embrace is a "together-hug with the Goddess and the God." As Wiccans, we understand death as a healing, a loving restoration rather than a punishing destruction. Any hurts or confusions there might have been in the body or in the mind are transformed.

We are challenged by death to see beyond the material plane, to resensitize our perception to other dimensions. Talk of Worlds "beyond the Veil" is not placebic platitude. There are other Worlds. They are accessible in many other cultures, and can be accessible in ours.

You can't see the wind, but you can feel its presence. You can't see loved ones whose bodies you have laid to rest, but you can feel their presence if you let yourself. You notice the wind's workings when you admire a sailing kite or find shapes in the clouds. You can notice the ways in which your loved ones affect the world, too, if you allow yourself to have that vision. But it is possible to bundle up so securely against the weather that you can't feel the wind. And it is possible to be so guilt-ridden and afraid of death that you can't perceive it as a part of life.

What the Goddess requires of you is not sacrifice, but trust, and you have already committed yourselves to that trust in your dedications and initiations. Her love is poured forth across the Lands—the spirit that animated your loved ones will be reborn, and through love and trust we will merry meet again in Her reunion.

These are complex feelings, and our perception of them has been distorted by an adversarial, authoritarian, patriarchal culture. Wiccans of various Traditions and experience need to come to a fearless, guiltless understanding of the relationship of death to life, each in their own ways. Culturally, death is still taboo. But if all acts of love and pleasure are Her rituals, and love unto all beings is Her law, then we have a moral obligation to the God/dess, to ourselves, and to our children to face the Guardian at that Gate.

In practical terms, it's a good idea to sort these things out before anyone is in mortal peril. If your family is part of a coven, suggest to your HPs an exploration of cultural and Wiccan attitudes toward death. A Circle to talk about your own death is interesting. Write your own epitaph, select your own music, imagine the site where you'd like your remains to rest. If your family circles alone, find times and places to talk about death. Mortality, remember, is not morbid, it's sacred, and is blasphemed by guilt and fear.

Should children take part in such exercises? Probably. You don't have to present the subject as harshly as the culture does. "What music do you think it would be nice to play when you go to greet the Gods?" you can ask. "When you move away from this World, what would you like your friends to remember about you?" If you think about it, you'll be able to ask questions like these, that won't scare your children and that will give them some sense of control over their lives and death.

When families talk about these things together, children learn other things, too. They learn, for instance, not to discount what you're saying just because you're crying when you say it. They learn that death is natural, sad but not bad. They learn that it's a good idea to take a look at your life now and then to remind yourself to live it the way you want. If you've talked about it before somebody dies, then none of you have to face your loss and the unknown at the same time. Also, you won't be as vulnerable to the Victorian inclination to pull away from each other in a crisis if you've practiced coming together.

If someone you love is dying, maybe you can give that person an opportunity to share some feelings, to ask some questions, to express some preferences. I can just about guarantee that you'll cry, but tears are cleansing—have a good cry, you'll feel better! And when you come right down to it, wouldn't you rather be with people who won't hide from the important feelings, instead of finding yourself alone at the end of your life, or when you're going through an intense phase?

You're *supposed* to have to summon up your courage to face death. Death is that transformation for which all others are preparatory. Death's path to rebirth is the adventure for which all mythical and legendary quests are metaphors. Can we bear it? Certainly we can, because the Goddess is with us, from the beginning and at the end of all desire.

Following—metaphorically—the advice Starhawk quoted, to follow the self to find the Self, we find that approaching our lives with reverence (and mirth) really does transform the mundane into the spiritual. Treating our ordinary lives with the same respect we give to our religious activities is one way to teach kids the sensitivity to perspective—attitude—that is so important in both realms.

(For a more in-depth exploration of this subject, see my book *In the Service of Life: a Wiccan Perspective on Death*, published by Kensington in 2003.)

Chapter Six

Moons and Suns

One of the things our family likes to do is camp. (Canyondancer was named for his skill in dancing an old Volkswagen bus through southern Arizona's canyons.) There are some beautiful places here in southeastern Arizona. What they call "sky islands," pine and oak forest oases, rise 5,000 to 9,000 feet from the desert floor, and we think they're perfect places to celebrate the Sabbats.

There may be wonderful places where you can camp, too; and there are, of course, a number of ways to camp. We've never been backpacking campers, for instance, though we've seen some entrancing photos of places you can only reach by carrying all your gear in. We've always been "car campers." We started with a small tent and then got a bigger one, and then for several years had Volkswagen campers, the self-contained pop-tops. Finally, we're opting for a small pick-up and a fold-out tent-trailer (which are named Puck the Silver Sprite and The Jewel of Sonora, respectively). We know people who enjoy sleeping on the ground, sometimes with just a blanket and not even a sleeping bag. The range of options is wide, and the pleasures of spending a few days in the "woo-ids" are not only great, we think, but brilliantly appropriate to all three major Neo-Pagan religions, Wicca, Asatru, and Druidry.

In our personal old days, we'd sit down every January with our calendar and choose the vacation days I'd take from work. Instead of taking my whole two weeks at once, we'd take a day here and two or three days there so we could camp a three- or four-day weekend more than once between Ostara and Samhain. We experimented with setting some of the year's Esbats in January, too, so we could arrange to be where we wanted to be for full Moons, and so the whole coven could be free on the same night. (This worked for a while, and then our members' work schedules fell right out of synch.)

If you can, try arranging your vacation schedule around the Sabbats and your family's favorite activities. It feels really good to reintegrate reverence, finding the sacred in the mundane. All acts of pleasure are Her rituals, and we honor Her with mirth as well as with reverence. Think about this next time you have some time off, and see what a nice guided tour the Goddess gives!

Moons

At our first covenstead the backyard was small. When we bought the apartment-sized rowhouse, the yard was hard dirt and the landscaping was construction debris. After 15 years, we had a circle of grass in an adobe patio, surrounded by woodsy rockeries, the makings of which had come home with us from camping trips.

Fallen branches, some of them livewood (with the tree spirit still in residence) decorated the cyclone fence. A cascading Tombstone rose arched up over the East, blooming like sunrise every Spring. In the buffer zone between the Circle and the carport, there were two garden boxes.

In one, our old Siamese cat and a pet rat were buried (their bones came with us when we moved) and catnip sprawled across the crystals that marked the graves.

Because our blood families lived in Oregon and the family cemeteries are there, the animals' graves in our yard stood for all the burial places of our people. When we wanted to, we could sit by those graves and commune with generations of ancestors, all the way back to Britain and Normandy, all the way back to the caves. Whether or not you've buried pets in your back yard, so can you. You can set up an "ancestor shrine" anywhere.

Adobe brick Altars stood at the North and South of our wild-growing grass Circle. At the South, there was a redwood ramada, where we fired up the Weber bonfire when we needed ritual flames. This Circle was the center of our first covenstead, and it was there that we usually observed the Moons.

One summer, the three of us were at Sunset Crater (between Flagstaff and the Grand Canyon) at a full Moon. A few miles from our site in the National Monument's campground, we found a clearing to cast our Circle. Lava gravel rolled beneath our feet, 15-foot lava cliffs jutted starkly up against a clear sky, and in the moonlight, lithe silver-white aspen, leaves dancing, shimmered. Our music and voices were the only other sounds— even the night birds were quiet.

We were so moved and inspired by that experience that we took several opportunities after that to move our Moon Circles into the desert around Tucson. Faerie Moon used to live a few miles beyond the city, and sometimes we'd hike a few minutes from her front door and cast our Circle on a low hill. Her beautiful husky, Banshee, used to come along, and enjoyed the rite as much as we did.

At our Moons, we do magic. Sometimes we do candle magic, maybe burning a small beeswax candle and chanting until it's gone, or letting it burn far enough to release a needle or disk inserted into the pillar. Usually we chant or sing; our chants are sometimes traditional, and sometimes not. "All we are saying/is give [peace, Earth, love, health, life] a chance" is still one we like to use.

We work for ourselves and each other, and for our friends who've asked or given their permission, and for the world. (We don't need anyone's permission to work for peace on Earth or an end to pollution or a decrease in the crime rate. Peace, a clean environment, and crime-free societies will not impede any true wills.) Sometimes we work for love, sometimes for health, sometimes for success. Faerie Moon used to bring her special poppy-seed bread, and I think our magic worked better when she baked it for Cakes and Ale.

Although our coven worked much more casually later on, we used to wear black robes, without hoods, for Esbats; we're still barefoot as often as reasonable caution allows. (Stepping on scorpions or cactus spines is not required, but we don't let gravel or a few twigs daunt us.) The Explorer wore his pentacle, Canyondancer often wore a gold ankh that was a gift from an English Witch, and I wore special crystals or other stones, to charge them or to call upon their power.

Sometimes we did other Moons, usually new, with other Witches, often in secluded areas of public parks. Using the Witches' Rune, we'd dance on drawings in the sand, or raise sound energy and direct it for healing one of our number. At these street-clothed, candle-less gatherings, we practiced new Quarter calls or invocations, and tried out new ways of working; and we usually shared pot-luck feasts when the work was done.

You might need to do something less obvious. A picnic dinner in the park and a conversations about the beginnings you'd like to work on—projects you're starting or habits you're forming—can be a proper new Moon. It's up to you! Children's energy is naturally suited to new Moon work, of course, for children are just beginning, too.

By the way, if you're new to Wicca, you may be wondering about how, exactly, a Moon Circle—or a Sabbat (Sun) Circle is conducted. Well, there are plenty of books out there that explain it—including a couple of mine, which I'm naturally going to recommend. Appendix A of *Celebrating the Seasons of Life: Samhain to Ostara* gives you step-by-step instructions, which you can follow or modify. And Appendix A of *Celebrating the Seasons of Life: Beltane to Mabon* is about casting Circles in your living room, in case you're an urban Wiccan without access to a private backyard or a safe park. Both books were published in 2004 by New Page Books, and both are filled with even more rituals and activities you can share with your family.

Suns

We used to meet for Sabbats (which we often call "Suns") and Esbats with our coven—years ago, Faerie Moon and her then-husband, the Norseman, were its charter members with us. Since then, the coven's had more and fewer members, cycling through the years like any family. Every year we've celebrated at least one Sabbat in the woods. We've always planned for three—at least three Sabbats, each for three nights—but plans have to be flexible; yours are probably flexed as often as ours were and still are. Since Campsight disbanded, its successor coven, Hearth's Gate, is the official host of our "Sabbat Villages," but the population hasn't changed much.

It seems to us that the rules for successful camping—plan ahead, be ready for rain, leave the site cleaner than you found it, and so on—are pretty good rules for living anywhere. In town, between the Worlds, anywhere. (Our coven, the Adventure Tradition's first, was named afer this way of seeing things, "camp sight.")

For the last 17 years (or more, depending on when you read this) we've celebrated Beltane with a camping trip to a different site almost every year—once or twice we've been to the same place two years in a row, and sometimes we've been back to a site a few years later. I've always been willing to hold most Sabbats on the closest weekend, but for many years, I insisted on celebrating Beltane on the first of May. In 1991, when May first was a Wednesday, we had to make it a five-day weekend. Sadly, this has not always been possible; in 2003, our Beltane Village got pushed back to the weekend of May 10th!

Dancing a Maypole with only five people, as we did our first year, is hard: you really need an even number of people. To ensure that we'd have an even number of dancers, we started inviting other Wiccans to share Beltane with us. Believe me, a Maypole's much better with 16 dancers than with five! For a few years, Beltane Village was open to any and all members of the Tucson Area Wiccan-Pagan Network (TAWN); later, with a core group established, the Village population was limited to the Camping Contingent and their vouched-for guests.

Many another camper, and a ranger or two, has seen and heard our revels, and you know what? No one's ever bothered us. Not even the officers at the inspection station on the Arizona/New Mexico border ever questioned the Maypole lashed to the Jeep's luggage rack. One year, rangers at the Chiricahua National Monument told us we couldn't leave the 'pole up in the meadow overnight, as we usually did, because Girl Scouts were coming, and might be alarmed or offended! When they said we couldn't use the meadow again, either, we just crossed that site off our list.

It was disappointing, but it wasn't an ugly confrontation, and we think it was the Girl Scouts' loss. (Indeed, one of the children in our group is now a "junior Girl Scout," a Brownie, and dancing the Children's Maypole for several years doesn't seem to have warped her in the least!) But Beltane's not the only Sabbat, and we celebrate all of them in ways we hope to share with any grandchildren we have.

Yule

When 'dancer and I were growing up, Christmas was the same every year. Times have changed, though, and now our Yules are a little different every year. We do keep some traditions, though. A bright 13-inch paper tree that my aunt decorated for us with Mexican paper flowers, straw birds, and other tiny treasures comes out every year. (The fondly remembered "fairy spinner" that chimes delicately when its small candles heat the air and turn the whirler has stayed in its box the last few years because it proves too attractive to the cats.)

For the Explorer's first Yule, we bought him a stocking we found at a craft fair, appliquéd with a cloth elf that looked just like the boy. We still have it, but we don't use it anymore because now we use little *cauldrons* instead of stockings. I bought several of them at an after-Halloween sale one year, and I fill them with stocking—er, I mean, cauldron-stuffers.

Some presents go under the tree, but we put most of them in one of our big plastic cauldrons. We open presents from the little cauldrons before breakfast, recalling one of my family's traditions. We used to open the rest during Cakes and Ale, but in the last decade, our Yule celebrations have expanded to include many noncoveners, so now on Yule morning we have a family hour, and then a coven hour, which we now share with Hearth's Gate, before people—some Pagan, some not—start arriving for the open house.

Our Yule Circle is now open to our friends and any guests they're willing to vouch for. We ask Wiccans of other Traditions, as well as Druids and Asatruar who are there, to call Quarters, and we have different men taking the roles of the Oak and Holly Kings every year. Our ritual also requires a Narrator and a Maiden, and these roles, too, are often filled by guests, who get 3 × 5 cards with their lines printed out. There are costumes for each role, too, and every player is merrily cheered by an enthusiastic peanut gallery. We're fortunate to have a large Circle at what is now the Traditionstead, so the Kings have plenty of room to battle dramatically, which they do with more style every year.

Cakes and Ale is shorter than usual, because everyone's looking forward to the pot-luck feast inside. We do use alcohol now, and those who don't wish to taste any either anoint themselves with it or pour a small libation of it. And when the Circle's been opened, the HPs (that would be me!) rushes to the open French doors and braces herself, legs wide apart. As the other celebrants leave the Circle, they taste a fingertip of Salt from the Altar (salt for the "bitterness" of death) and are then, one at a time, reborn by crawling through the HPs' wide-spread legs. There's a small dish of honey to taste as people struggle to their feet again, honey for the sweetness of renewed life. And then there's the feast.

We still save a portion of the trunk of last year's Yule tree, and burn it—either in the chiminea (a Mexican clay fireplace) at the South in our Circle, or in the living room fireplace—and most years we have a Yule-log cake. The open-house, pot-luck feast generally goes on for several hours, with people who come later replenishing the food. We provide the Roast Beast, and everyone else provides the rest.

Bride (Brigid, Imbolc)

Candles made from various informal molds, includint goblets from the thrift store, fill an Altar at Bride.

We love candles, even if they do curl the cats' eyebrows. So at Bride, the ritual might be short, but the candles are tall, or at least many, and burn all evening, filling the house and yard with light and warmth like that of the returning Sun. We dress a Biddy and decorate a Wand, in a rite modified from the Farrars' in *A Witches Bible Compleat* (Magickal Childe Inc, 1987). We don't grow our own wheat, so we can't braid the Biddy from the last sheaf of last year's harvest. We use raffia, which the cats appreciate; maybe it makes up for the curled eyebrows.

It was also our tradition (and continues to be a personal observance) to burn the last of Yule's greenery at Bride. Each covener took a few dry branches, cut from the Yule tree and carefully saved, and tossed them into the Fire at South. Some would take a moment to mention, usually privately, any remnants of the Winter they wanted to be rid of, and let those go in the Fire, too. The flames are sometimes impressively high, yet the sumac, or pepper, tree that arches over the chiminea has never caught fire. (There's a garden hose right behind the Fire, ready just in case.) We take down any Yule decorations still out now, too, though thanks to the kitties, there aren't usually very many left.

Since 1999, we've celebrated a coven child's birthday at Bride, too, in a separate, less formal ritual written by her mother. Bride is (was) also Campsight's anniversary, so there was usually an extra bit of celebration, and now there's a little extra remembrance.

At Bride, we notice the lengthening hours of light, and on some February days, it's warm enough to open the back door in the afternoon. Part of our Bride ritual involves sweeping the Circle—"thus we banish Winter, thus we welcome Spring," and mundanely, we start our Spring Cleaning at this time of year, too. When he lived with us, the Explorer shared the Spring Cleaning chores, and your kids can share as much or as little of your Bride rites as you think is appropriate.

Ostara

Sometimes it's still chilly when we camp at Ostara, but we're ready by then to get out in the woods again, so we go anyway. Most years we take egg-dying kits with us. One year, when we had colored all the eggs we'd brought, there was dye left over, so the Explorer colored pale rocks and peeled twigs, too! We usually have an egg hunt for the kids. There's almost every year been a "gift from the Goddess," too (a special sighting of wild-life, for instance, or spectacular pictures that surprise us when the film's developed).

You can take your eggs and dye to a local park or out in the yard. If using real eggs for a hunt is impractical (we always count 'em first, and after the kids bring 'em back, and in the meantime try really hard to remember where we hid them), use the plastic ones that come apart. Try filling them with runes on colored paper. You can hide decorative wooden eggs, too, or ones you cut from our friend, construction paper.

The stores are full of Easter cards and decorations. We remember all the little girls in our old neighborhoods—where we lived when the Explorer was young, and where Canyondancer and I lived as children—being frilled up in new pink and purple dresses and shiny white shoes, and the little boys sporting sharp suits with hankies in their pockets. Moms dress up their kids while our Mother dresses up the Earth in leaf and bud.

In some areas of the country, Ostara would be almost as subtle as Bride but for the mainstream's Easter festivities. This is a great time to talk about history, about fertility and rebirth, the youth of the year and the growth to come. With older children and cowan family members and friends, Ostara can be an appropriate time to explore a variety of reli-gious metaphors and symbolism. Thoughts as well as baby chicks can be hatched. (Speaking of baby chicks and bunnies, don't give live ones as Ostara gifts. Plush are better.)

Beltane

Our Maypole lived in the ramada at our first covenstead, in the eaves of our shed at the second. The first Adventure Maypole was retired after 10 years of service, and the second one is nearing the end of its term.

(When it retires, Hearth's Gate will find, prepare, and tend the next one.) Now the first two live under the eave of our carport. We no longer carry the the 'pole to camp lashed to the Jeep's luggage rack, but it was visible through the windows of the VW camper we drove for several years. Now, alas, it travels invisibly in the pop-up trailer; but we still have a wreath decorating the back of the vehicle.

For a few years, we exchanged Beltane gifts the way we exchange Yule gifts. Now what we do is ask everyone who plans to dance to bring an inexpensive but entertaining gift, gaily wrapped, to put under the May-pole. Then, during Cakes and Ale, we each choose a present other than the one we brought (trades are allowed) and enjoy these gifts from the Goddess and God. We also use two Maypoles now, because the truth is that until they're age 8 or 9, kids don't dance the 'pole correctly. This really bugged me, until we made a Maypole especially for the children.

My theory is that it doesn't matter if children tangle up their own Maypole; children's energy is supposed to be a bit wild, and they're not wholly responsible for their lives yet. But when we put them in charge of a ribbon on the adults' 'pole, their erratic energy disrupts ours, and we can't control even our own ribbons as well as we should. The Maypole comes out lumpy, and so, often as not, do our lives throughout the next few months.

The first time we let the kids dance their own 'pole, the grown-ups were delighted to be able to watch the children frolic without having to dodge them (many of them are really too short to dance with us, too—it's hard to go under a ribbon held by someone barely 3 feet tall!). There were agonized moans of sudden revelation when the kids were done, too: "Oh, Goddess, is that what *our* Maypole looks like? No wonder our lives are so messed up!" Yes, things are going much better now.

Maybe it's the exception that proves the rule. In most matters, Wiccans protest that there isn't just "one right way," but there is, indeed, one right way to dance the Maypole. We believe it's important to dance the 'pole properly, and the "Instructions" that we read before we turn on the music explains it pretty well:

> The magic of the Maypole's in the braiding of the strands.
>
> These ribbons are our futures, and we hold them in our hands.
>
> The more that we are careless, the greater life's demands:
>
> dance badly, you'll climb mountains; dance well, and walk on sand.
>
> With beauty and with strength, with power and compassion,
>
> with honor and humility, reverent dance, in mirthful fashion!
>
> Over and under, again and again, weaving the Web's connections.
>
> Ribbons tight! Pattern sure! And *do not* change directions!

Canyondancer hung the grown-ups' Maypole over the table so we could enjoy the ribbons' colors, even though there were so few adults that we only danced the Children's 'Pole.

We have favorite Maypole music that we play every year on our portable "boom box," though some years we were blessed with live bagpipe music. *Music from the Hearts of Space*, broadcast on our classical station, is our main source of Sabbat music, though there are lots of specifically

Pagan tapes available. We dress festively for the Maypole in long skirts, tunics, and garlands in our hair—one year the Explorer wore a wizard's hat! And yes, the Great Rite has been performed, for the woods where we go are both sacred and private (and all of us know about tents).

What we try to do at Beltane, while we're removed from the city's concerns and can live in our Mother's house for a few days, is recreate a sense of old community. We become a little village of tents (some owned, some rented or borrowed; the one we used for years was called May Hall, our first VW camper was called Bag End, and the second was named Rainbow's End); a little Circle of hearth fires.

We have to chop wood and carry water and work at our comfort, just like in the old times. We used to have at least one communal feast, and a stone soup to which everyone contributed a little something; now we're more likely to get together for a snack of French bread and Brie. We still have the Bel Fire, after the Maypole, after the Sword and Wreath Toss, at which the trophy competition is delight-fully fierce; and 'round the Bel Fire, we still share our newly-written verses of *Old Time Religion*.

Some years we still leap the Fire, too, but sometimes the Forest Service fire-places are constructed so as to make that dangerous; in that case, we just step over them, or settle for being well-smoked when the wind in the canyon changes with the coming of darkness. If you want to leap a Fire, think about a grouping of tea lights on the lawn; if you'd like (or need) to do something even less athletic, try strolling with your sweetie between two candles.

2002's trophies for 1st and 2nd place in the Sword and Wreath Toss and the best new verse to Old Time Religion.

Litha

Not all of us have children, nor are all our children the same age. But while camping or in town, everybody cares for all the kids, giving them time, attention, and affection, sharing our Wiccan values and showing them our joy. If we're at camp, our ritual is low key and varies to take advantage of the campground. If we're in town, we may keep the Sabbat with other Tucson Witches (TAWN sponsors open Sabbat rituals led by various members, and the local ADF Druids of the Sonoran Sunrise Grove hold open rituals at every Sabbat, too). Sometimes we just Circle at the Traditionstead, with Campsight's successor coven, Hearth's Gate, and then we might have a Kings' Battle (mirroring the one at Yule) or light a Sun Wheel and roll it into a small pool.

In 1990, one of Tucson's very gifted priestesses, Sue Bond, whose children were young then, introduced a wonderful new element to our repertoire: the Sun Pole. It rose out of the tree stand from the middle of a circle of 50 of us, and we hung tokens of our joy upon it. One woman hung a feather, symbolic of the freedoms she gave up to be a mommy and the freedoms she enjoys in motherhood. The ceremony moved many of us to tears, and has not been forgotten. Can you adapt it for your family?

At Litha, we're celebrating abundance, full strength, "the prime." Everything is at its height, yet our appreciation of the height is only possible from an awareness of depth. A re-enactment of the Oak and Holly Kings' Battle, Holly victorious and reigning till Yule, keeps things in perspective. Children lend an appropriately gleeful confidence, battling with wrapping-paper-tube swords and full-throated cries of sheer aliveness.

(There are lots of swords available in stores now—*Star Wars* swords and Frodo's sword, Sting, in addition to the ones you can buy for Halloween costumes. These are more appropriate for older kids or grown-ups, though: don't waste a younger child's power of imagination, when it can make a decorated cardboard sword so real; don't deny a kid the exercise of that imagination, either. There's time for fancier props later.)

Lammas (Lughnassad)

I used to work in an old Victorian house with a big yard, where on one of the fences there grew a vine. It might have been Bleeding Heart, or it might have been Queen's Wreath; I was never sure, and either was appropriate. Every year I made a Vine God from it. Since I retired, I've used raffia, and grapevine figures. I like the variety, but I kind of miss the old way.

Sometime in late June, I'd take two large paper cups and tape the open ends together. Then, on a lunch hour, I'd go outside, and after asking nicely and saying thanks, I'd cut some long strands of that vine and start winding. I'd make a loop for the head, and made horns, too, though we'd sometimes have to take it on faith that one protrusion or another was a horn. The arms and legs were easier.

I dried Him on a shelf in my office. Every year I wrote a little note of explanation:

In case you're wondering, this is a Vine God. He represents the grain and fruit that nourish us all. At the first Harvest Festival, around the first of August, we will fill him with cornbread and then let Him die on a fire, as fruits and grains ripen every year and die in the harvest so we can live. When the Vine God has been consumed, the cornbread will be left, and we will share it in a communion honoring life's cycles.

The people I worked with were Catholic, Protestant, and Jewish, and they were always interested and respectful, and once they'd read the note, they thought it was "cool."

When it was time, I'd take the Vine God home; sometimes 'dancer would come and pick me up, but sometimes, the God rode the bus home with me. (That gave me another chance to play show-and-tell, and I always enjoyed it.) On Lammas Night, 'dancer usually makes a special dinner, usually acorn squash with sausage stuffing (now, since his heart attack and triple bypass, it's fat-free sausage, which is not so bad, actually).

Murchadh prepares a grapevine-and-raffia Vine God for a Lammas rite.

And we always have cornbread and strawberries. These days, Hearth's Gate makes the Vine God, and He looks different every year, which is just as it should be.

You can make a Vine God, too, and fill him with heavy duty foil-wrapped cornbread—the paper cups come out to make a place for it. Watch Him go up in the proverbial blaze of glory on your Weber bonfire. When He's gone, like grain from the fields and fruit from the vine, unwrap the cornbread (look out—it's hot!) bless it, and share it. At dinner afterwards, talk about the harvest and how it works in the Worlds and in your lives.

Mabon

Tucson's annual and public Fall Festival and Faire, sponsored by TAWN, attracts several hundred people, our family circle among them. It was a cauldron-luck, and is still a real community celebration of the harvest. Everyone brings the kids, and some years, until its time for the ritual, we have to look out for frisbees!

We collect donations for the Community Food Bank, and the workers there know about TAWN, and appreciate Tucson's Pagans' contributions.

As I began work on this revision, TAWN's annual Fall Fest was just a couple of months off, and we were honored that the rehearsals for the open Mabon ritual were held here, at what was then still Campsight's covenstead. Some Fall Fests have been held at the local Unitarian-Universalist Church because the cost of insurance for a public festival in the park has been beyond us. The Church's coffee hall and courtyards were smaller spaces, and facilitated even more intimate rituals.

We think it's important to do public ritual for several reasons. It lets our children realize that what we do is not just a family tradition, but a world-wide human tradition. When kids see a couple of hundred people from all over Southern Arizona gathered together, it's easy for them to accept that there are gatherings like this in other cities, too.

At Fall Fest, our children see the many Traditions of Wicca, and of other Neo-Pagan faiths, and their outward expressions and symbols—coven banners, Earth flags, drums, dress robes, and the like. And in the sometimes-huge ritual Circle, they can get some feel for our lore's great Sabbats of old, when hundreds of Witches, coveners, and solitaries, gathered to observe our Rites in Common.

That's not to mention the good that public ritual does for Wicca's public image. The Fall Festival at Mabon doesn't have to compete with other public holidays (okay, one year we goofed up and scheduled it for the same weekend as the Street Fair, but we learned our lesson about that!), and with "Halloween" coming up, our openness helps sensitize people. It also makes the often thankless task of public education a lot more fun.

At home, we used to weave Cords of Life, something we learned from Starhawk's Mabon ritual in *The Spiral Dance*. We haven't done that for some time, but Cords from many years hung in our ramada, and reminded us to consider our personal harvests every year.

Samhain

Faerie Moon used to host a secular costume party every year, and we loved to dress up and go. We hosted a Samhain rite at the covenstead for a few years, and then we started celebrating at camp. For a long time, we held the rite on October 31st, but in recent years, we've deferred to other parents' preference to be home on that night, so their children could trick-or-treat. But in 'dancer's and my old days, covenstead celebrations were at midnight, and rites in the woods were on the 31st. (I almost always took the following Monday off work, and if the 31st was a school day, we kept the Explorer out.)

There are lots of great ritual sites in Southeastern Arizona, but we have settled upon one for Samhain, and we've been going there for almost two decades now. Of course, camping in cold weather (and having a good time at it) requires some careful planning, and most of Samhainville's regular residents have got it down pretty well now. Camp comfortably set up, there's nothing like a dark, chilly, and nonordinary environment to give you a head start on understanding what Samhain is all about. The scariest movies and commercial haunted houses pale by comparison. We think Samhain in the "woo-ids" is just about the most fun a Witch can ever have!

Several carved pumpkins and an elf-light anchor this community Samhain Altar on a campground table.

Carrying our lit jack o' lanterns (there's a prize for the one the group likes best) we process from the group camp to the ritual site, where we use the glowing pumpkins as "Quarter Jacks." In our ritual, we light candles for our dead, and emphasize Nature's demonstrations that all of life is part of the cycle, and comes back.

As above, so below. The constellations are not stationary in our skies, nor are they erratic. No, they cycle 'round and 'round, rolling with the seasons. So do we. You can't create or destroy energy—this is the first law of physics, and it holds true for all energy. From a Wiccan perspective, this means it's reasonable to expect that energy released by death will be transformed to new life.

Beyond death, I give peace, and freedom, and reunion with those who have gone before, the Goddess promises. Commonly, we understand "those who have gone before" to mean people we know who have died, but "those who have gone before" are also loved ones who have "gone" back to the physical plane. In the Summerland or reincarnated, we believe with many other Wiccans that "reunion" means a joining with all the family groups we have built through the many generations.

The Veil is thin at Samhain, and not only between the Worlds. The distinctions between past and present fade, between tribe and nuclear family. When all the ancestors come to Samhain's family reunion, those of us incarnate at the moment feel the nurturing embrace of all our generations, and it is just as warm as the Sun in high Summer. While the Explorer was young, we focused on Samhain as a family reunion, and the new year; and we still do.

When my mother died a few years ago, I followed the Victorian custom of making a funeral wreath and hanging it on the front door. I left it there for a month or so, and then saved it—and burned it at Samhain. It decorated our camp—Samhainville—for three days, and I invited people to write messages on 3 x 5 cards, and tuck them into the grapevine twines and under the ribbons that decorated Mom's wreath.

Children and grown-ups alike wrote notes to their answers, some drew pictures, and some tucked in more than one message. We burned it in the morning fire on our last day, and watched our love, respect, and messages cross over in the smoke. Since then, the Funeral Wreath has become a belovéd custom, one I expect to follow even if there's ever a year we don't camp for Samhain; and it's certainly a mini-rite that can be managed in many ways, even with construction paper if grapevine's unavailable.

The Practical Side

In addition to marking the Sabbats religiously, we observe them practically, too. In Arizona, the Sun dominates our lifestyle. His course through the year determines when we open which blinds and what windows to take best advantage of the weather. I used to notice the differences at the bus stop, too: between Beltane and Samhain, I didn't need a coat! The shadow of the bus stop sign moved about 5 feet along the ground from Yule to Litha. And of course, the Explorer could play outside longer (by Litha, it's light until almost 10 p.m., and that's without daylight savings!).

These are things every family can notice. Even if you can't observe the Sabbats with Wicca's full religious glory, you can take a nature walk through your neighborhood. You can go to the planetarium; if there isn't one where you live, there might be one at the closest university, and it might be worth going the four times a year that most planetariums put on seasonal shows. You can visit local museums and libraries, too. All of them will have relevant shows sometime. Botanical gardens and zoos sometimes do, too.

A project that can be of interest for children and adults is making a Wheel of the Year. It can be as simple or as elaborate as your tastes and budget run. On nature walks, or when you're at the park or camping, you can pick up leaves, small rocks and twigs, feathers, and other souvenirs of the wild. From colorful magazine pages or construction paper, you can cut out other symbols of the Sabbats. You may find some appropriate illustrations in your computer's graphics program, too. With an inexpensive bottle of glue, you can fasten these things to a Wheel you've made with string, yarn, or construction paper, and paste it to a piece of poster board or length of material.

Among other things you might use on such a Wheel are pictures of clouds and other weather symbols cut out of the paper or magazines, small shells, bells, ribbons, tiny paper chains, silk leaves and blossoms, and so on. Wrapping paper often has neat images on it, too. In the middle, you might like to use drawings you or your children have made of the Goddess and God.

The Wheel you make will be a fine backdrop to your Altar. It's an excellent teaching device as well, for you can use it to show your kids (and maybe friends or relatives) the relationships between the seasons and our holidays. And in making it, you'll learn a lot about the way the seasons affect your lives. You'll be reminded that seasons are not our invention, but like the grain and game that die annually, were here long before we humans grew up, and will be here when we have all been transformed.

As your Wheel of the Year becomes an heirloom, its corners bent, its decorations reglued a hundred times, it will become a symbol of the Gods Themselves. Though the decorations and pictures you make it with may tear and fold and fade, the Wheel itself remains, reborn with every new illustration, every new decoration, every loving repair. Just so are we renewed in every cycle, transformed every day.

Don't forget food, either. Like families of other faiths, we have special foods for holidays. Children can help from young ages, and special Sabbat recipes can become treasured family heirlooms; booklets of recipes and the family and/or coven stories behind them can be gifts at passage rites. We used to like to vary our holiday menus from year to year.

However, since 'dancer's heart problems began to manifest and we've been following a fairly strict low-cholesterol, low-fat diet, we've standardized our Sabbat Feasts and look forward to them as times when we can legitimately break our diet!

Try Scott Cunningham's *The Magic in Food* (Llewellyn, 1991), and other sources for Sabbat fare. Check your own cookbooks, and maybe even your local newspaper, as well as online sites—and don't forget to ask your friends! (You can also refer to a few recipes in my two volumes of *Celebrating the Seasons of Life*: *Samhain to Ostara* and *Beltane to Mabon*.)

Deck the Halls!

Most families like to decorate for the holidays; we usually do the house and the car. But finding Wiccan decorations can be a challenge, even if we can use many of the same garlands and ornaments that everybody else does.

We've found that right after Christmas, there are a lot of Beltane decorations on sale, although the stores selling them at half-price or less probably don't know that's what they can be. Lights and tinsel in a variety of colors are marked down, and so are ornaments, many of which are suitable for Beltane, Litha, and even Ostara. During Campsight's final year, we got Sabbat tokens for our members—and we found the ones for Ostara, Litha, and Yule on sale after Christmas. The cottony white squares decorated with multi-colored glitter, sold for Christmas tree skirts, make fine Maypole skirts, too.

Bells, colored glass balls, stars (occasionally pentagrams!), and faeries (they call them angels)—all of these, along with bead and "evergreen" garlands—are appropriate to several of our holidays. Even those things which are too Yule-ish to use at any other time can be used in ways the cowan would never imagine: candle wreaths of silk fir, pin, or holly, for example, make great crowns for battling kings, as do tinsel and silk garlands. If you go to a craft store after Christmas, Easter, and Halloween, you'll find lots of decorations and accessories for the Sabbats.

We like to make decorations, too. Some years we make paper chains at Yule; at Ostara, we've decorated eggshells (blow out the contents and have scrambled eggs) which we can then string or hang by pipe cleaners. We've used wrapping paper tubes to make miniature Maypoles; decorated with tin foil or colored paper and ribbons, we've used them for Kings' swords, too.

With ribbons and other pretty scraps and a block of florist's foam or Styrofoam shapes that any craft store carries, even a small child can make a centerpiece or headpiece. Putting the decoration in a small cauldron and tying the cauldron with a bright ribbon will brighten up a table, mantle, or corner at a Sabbat. A larger plastic cauldron will hold a punch bowl, too, and decorated with a bow or other ornaments—strings of plastic pearls or other beads around the rim are nice—it's a neat way to serve up any brew. (At Samhain, you might want to add dry ice, though you can't let children mess with it on their own because it can burn their fingers.) You might be able to stand a short or decorative Maypole or a small Yule tree in a large cauldron, too. They're too big even for the largest cauldron, but "Christmas tree" stands hold our adults' and the children's Maypole, too.

Faerie Moon was the first of us to find a 6-foot twig broom at a craft fair, and she kept it, bristles up, beside her massive stone fireplace. She decorated it with tiny colored lights and seasonal baubles, and everyone loved it. You can make a Yule broom if you can't have a real or artificial tree, too. We used to use a white-painted and be-ribboned flat, fan-shaped broom to mark the site of our annual Beltane, too. "Look for the White Broom," the reminders we mailed would say.

Do we have to wait for a Sabbat to decorate? Not at all! We don't even have to wait for birthdays, anniversaries, graduations, passages, our teams' championships, or company, either. Our homes can be festive year-round.

Winter is cold even in Arizona, and houses can be drafty. In the "old days," tapestries and other wall hangings blunted the chill, and they can today, too. You can hang a wall with quilts or curtains or even area rugs. Brick veneer or real wood paneling can evoke the feeling of ancestral halls.

Fireplaces can be decked with seasonal garlands or bouquets; mantles can be subtle altars, for many a mantle figure (museum reproductions, for instance) is Pagan. Charms can be disguised as mainstream crafts, if disguise is necessary, and displayed on a mantle, bookshelf, or table. (Those of us with cats can set such spells to release their magic when curious paws knock them *off* the mantle! That's one way to work *with* nature.)

If you know your ethnic heritage, you can bring it home in your choice of furniture styles or colors. "Regional" colors here include a forest green, common as well to Celtic decoration. We enjoy being able to conjure up our own cultural heritage, keeping right in vibrant Southwest style at the same time. There are color choices even for apartment walls, and one thing almost anyone can do is coordinate wall colors with Quarter colors. We don't necessarily recommend painting each wall of a room a different color; but three walls neutral and one wall a directional color might be nice.

Windows can be decorated (and not merely covered) with curtains, and they're easy to make. The clerks at most fabric stores will help you, or you can get one of many how-to books. All you really need to do is be able to sew a straight seam—and if you don't have a sewing machine, you can get some hem tape that will let you make a seam with only an iron! Wreaths and garlands are nice on windows, too.

Tablecloths are also easy to make. For most rectangular tables, all you need is two yards of any fabric you like. Cut 12 inches off one end (cut that strip in quarters and you have four napkins; leave it long and you have a runner or an Altar cloth, all of which need only narrow hemming). The tablecloth needs hemming only on the two short ends; the sides are selvage edges and can be left as they are. These can be inexpensive enough to make one for every Sabbat and another for the Moon, if you like.

They're just the right size to completely cover a 47-quart cooler, too, turning it into a portable Altar with storage space for Tools and Cakes and Ale, as long as you don't mind a chilled handle on your athame. I've used the cloth-covered cooler as an Altar for the rituals I used to demonstrate to local church groups; it's handy and it works better than a cardboard box.

Archways and interior doors are good places for curtains and swags or garlands, and doors (even pocket doors!) take posters or paint. In the bathroom, you have the same freedom with your shower curtain as you do with tablecloths, for you can make your own with any fabric you like. The easiest way? Buy a clear or solid-colored plastic shower curtain, measure it, buy fabric to cover it, and use spray adhesive to glue the fabric to one side of the shower curtain. You can also decorate the plastic curtain with designs cut out from fabric, or with designs you cut from self-adhesive shelf paper, or with painted designs.

If you want to sew a shower curtain, measure the curtain bar and add 18 inches to the measurement. Measure the length from the curtain bar to the floor, and add 3 inches. Then do some figuring: how much material you'll need depends on the fabric width. You'll have to sew a center seam to get a piece big enough, and you'll need extra fabric to match plaids and some other patterns.

The edges will be selvage and won't need a hem. At the top and bottom, make a 1 1/2-inch hem. At the top, through both layers of fabric, make 12 button-holes, evenly spaced. If you have a machine, the button-holer will work; otherwise, grommets may work, but be sure they're big enough to fit over the hooks on your shower rod. The bottom of the curtain should fall somewhere between an inch and a quarter inch off the floor. Of course, the fabric stays outside the tub at all times; the plastic liner goes inside. If your bathroom has a window, use any left over fabric to make curtains. Sometimes it's okay to be a "designer Witch."

Another way to decorate your house (no matter what the season) is with the mini-lights they sell for Winter holidays. You can hang crystals in your windows, too, or paint delicate designs on the edges or in the corners with tempera paints. (This is a wonderful family Sabbat project for sliding glass doors, or on an inclement or recovering-from-something afternoon, and clean up isn't too bad.)

Coven banners are great fun to make, and your coven doesn't have to be large, or rich, to hang one. The Wiccan community here is fairly public, so we see banners at most gatherings; the Tucson Area Wiccan-Pagan Network has one, too, that flies every month at the "cauldron-luck" in the park.

At a discount fabric store, Faerie Moon and I found oversized sample squares that became the field for Campsight's first banner. I sewed four of them—same pattern, different colors—together for the background, which measured about two feet by four feet. In the center we wanted an obvious symbol of Witchcraft, and decided on a cauldron. I cut a large one out of black cotton, leaving a collar like edge at the top. I put a circle of batting down, and a smaller one on top of it, so the cauldron would be in soft bas-relief. Over a narrow strip of batting, I rolled the cauldron's collar down so it had the depth of a real cauldron's rim. I used my sewing machine to sew down the bowl of the cauldron, but I finished the rim by hand.

An arching arrangement of "silk" leaves and branches went just above the cauldron, as its handle. The greenery extended about an inch beyond the sides of the banner, so the leaves could rustle a bit in the breeze. Below the cauldron was a triple Moon, cut from a flexible mirror-like material, the like of which I never found again (a banner I made just a couple of years later used tin foil instead). The two crescents and the full circle were glued down, and edged with glittery fabric paint. The Explorer made the choice of the "rainbow" glitter paint from among several colors we had on hand.

At left, Campsight Coven's second banner. At right, a computer "sketch" of an Adventure Tradition banner.

Beneath all the symbols and decorations were the words CAMPSIGHT COVEN spelled out on two centered lines. The letters (from a local craft store) were made of wood, painted black, and edged with a metallic copper paint. Copper is not an especially traditional Wiccan material, but it is a traditional material here in the Southwest, and now is popular elsewhere. The beads on the end of the 3-foot long black dowel on which the banner hung were glued in place, and they were banded with copper, too.

We also used a length of purple leather cord to hang it. In the house, the dowel rested on two nails, but in a park or at camp, we couldn't count on finding two branches close enough together, so the hanging cord came in handy.

The finished banner was dedicated when we formalized the coven. But before it was officially consecrated, it was made with Celtic music— Gwyddion Pendragon, mostly—playing to it in the background. While I was absorbed in the handwork, the banner went with my imagination to the hills of Ireland, Scotland, and Wales, waving over leprechaun and fairy feasts. It held its own magic as well as what we gave it when we dedicated it.

The Explorer was somewhat indifferent about the banner while I was making it. The project took up most of the back room and my time for a few evenings. But once it was done, he was as proud of it as we were. Since then, the poor thing fell apart, and Campsight has a new banner (for which I used some of the old greenery, and the same design). The "new" banner—itself now several years old—is made of felt, but the cauldron's still dimensional. And the Explorer still has considerable respect for my graphics sense and crafting ability.

So, don't wait to decorate! The spirit is with us all the time: the God greets us every morning, the Goddess every evening. They do so much to make the world homey for us that we enjoy making our little corner homey for Them.

Elf Lights

Several years ago, Faerie Moon created what she calls "elf lights," and camping by ourselves or with others, we've used them ever since. To tell you how to make your own, here's Faerie Moon herself, excerpted from the Aprés-Ostara, 1990 issue of *The Celtic Camper*, a quarterly newsletter we used to print.

I easily recall the first one I built while we were camped on the edge of a huge meadow in the White Mountains. Dinner was barely finished when the dark started to bubble forth a summer storm. My husband hustled about securing things, and I began to fret about how to save the pretty votive candles I had flickering at the boundaries of our camp.

The moist wind was threatening to snuff them, and suddenly I began to bank the closest votive with some handy, flat, fist-sized rocks. Stacking them so that odd gaps allowed the colored light through, I capped the top of the little cairn with one long, slender piece of rock to fully shield the flame.

Inspired, I rushed to do the same for about four other votives. Luckily, plenty of rocks were available, and the ground had been cleared of flammable wisps of grass beforehand. The storm finally hit, dousing two of the lights, but the remaining ones shone bravely throughout! The rain was soon over, leaving an intoxicating damp green scent from the meadow. I relit the damaged votives and my husband and I settled back to enjoy the sensations.

After a few moments, my husband focused on the nearest stone cairn I had decorated with a couple of pine cones. "So just what do you call these?" he asked, interested.

"Elf lights," I answered before really thinking, although by instinct (Irish ancestry here) I knew that was what I had spontaneously built.

"What are they for?" My husband naturally asked this because he had learned that when Witches do such things, they usually mean something.

"Well, besides the fact that they keep us from tripping over the dark parts of our camp," I answered a bit smugly, "they form a protective area that invites the Wee Folk to come and bless our visit here inside their home. Sort of a respectful beacon, you might say."

Then we started to go camping with O'Gaea and Canyondancer and their son. Our first time out, I instructed them to gather many rocks (the flatter and more stackable, the better) and we began a tradition with them that continues to this day.

With other folks helping, the elf lights got fancier in spots, some nestled in rocks over the water, lit up like diminutive caves when the sun sank down. Others were placed in gnarled root grottos (carefully shielded with stones so as not to catch fire). Some were decorated with seasonal offerings or statues of gnomes, or given tiny crystal windows when we wedged clear quartz pieces in amongst the stones.

If you'd like to try elf light building (inside your home or out) there are a few important guidelines. The most important, of course, is safety: i.e., fire hazard. Some campgrounds, especially those patrolled by rangers, have strict fire codes, and you could be fined for any "open flame" outside your campfire.

Don't build where there's abundant dry grass or flammable dry branches. Clear elf light circumferences down to dirt, and select broad, flat stones for a fire-proof base for your votive candle *in a glass holder*. Then insulate the light, building up on all sides with rocks. Be cautious with decorations near the flame; make sure nothing can accidentally fall or blow in and catch fire. [O'Gaea's note:

these days, we sometimes use tea-lights, which come in protective metal holders, but we're still *very* careful. We still clear the area and use broad, flat stones underneath; we gather up the candles and clean up any leaked wax before we leave, too, even though we leave the cairns in place.]

Always use slats of thin rock to cap the cairn, several inches above the flame, for extra protection. Stagger the wall-rocks enough so the light will show through—and experiment with different colored glasses for different colors of light. Be innovative as well as practical in placing elf lights; they make excellent path markers, and of course, beautiful celebratory touches for your indoor facilities. Permanent elf lights can be erected in your own yard; they can be cemented in place, leaving the cap stone(s) loose for candle placement.

A close-up view of an elf-light shows a tea-light wick peeking through a gap in the stones. The light twinkles merrily through these spaces when the elf-lights are lit at night.

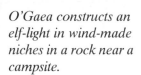

O'Gaea constructs an elf-light in wind-made niches in a rock near a campsite.

I've gone on Moon walks with several other Witches, and we've made elf lights to sit around and exchange stories or songs. These cozy little cairns provide an ancient Pagan link to the days of old, and are perfect to mark the directions when summoning Elementals. I even had them in my wedding circle!

So try elf lights, and sit back to watch the Wee Folks creep up next to the glittering mounds of stones. And always remember what Smokey (the obviously Pagan bear) says: Be careful with fire. Blesséd be, Campers!

When we've finished our elf lights, we build other things from twigs, bundles of pine needles, rocks, and fallen cones. We build castles and lodges, often softly telling the stories that go with them. (Stories are decorations, too, of the mind and of the spirit.) If there's wild water about, usually a small, rocky stream, we'll build pine-cone boats and rafts to sail in it. Stories come with some of them, too, and here's one of them:

The Antlered Oak Boat of Upper Herrin

Upper Herrin was so called to be distinguished from Herrin, which was an abandoned fishing village on the Grey Rock River. The Grey Rock River was so called because its course was lined with grey rocks, some of them pearly, some of them dark and time-smoothed.

It is not always necessary to build boats to fish from in a river; if your river is swift and narrow, it would be suicidal. Upper Herrin was about a mile upstream from Herrin, and farther than that from suicidal. It was a comfortable community, growing more and more wealthy from increasing enterprise. Upper Herrin did not need to build fishing boats. Upper Herrin needed to build tourist boats.

It was too dangerous to sail boats in the gorge along which Upper Herrin was built. But it was perfectly safe to moor boats permanently in the shoals to feed, house, and entertain tourists who came to see the quaint lifestyle of Upper Herrin, where they'd heard people lived in permanently moored boats.

To maintain tourist interest, Upper Herrin began to discover and share its history. Even though they made most of it up, one or two accuracies slipped by them. One of these accidental accuracies was that long, long ago, when old Herrin itself had been a mere circle of huts and a stick altar, Herriners had been hunters.

A dreadful fire in one season, followed by an incomparably cold winter, threatened them all. To save the people, the Horned One appeared to them as an enchanted hart, fully new-antlered at entirely the wrong time of year to be fully antlered. He led the astonished hunters to the river bank, where to their further astonishment, the hart strode into the water and bellowed a single note.

His voice called from one of the river-side oaks a tremendous shudder, and a large branch plummeted to the ground, striking the magical hart dead between the eyes. The hart's body then transformed itself, and what the stunned hunters saw at the end of their watching was an antlered leather boat with an oaken mast.

[Waterlogged bundles of pine needles, braided and woven around the ends of twigs, were the "leather" of the rafty boat I held in my hands; such transformation is, of course, not beyond the Horned One.]

So it was by this magical boat that the old Herriners were carried up the stream, and their rafts of belongings were pulled behind the Antlered Oak Boat to the place that became Upper Herrin. Generations later, finding their living so easy to make in the abundance to which the God had led them, they had quite a lot of leisure time, which they filled first by constructing a studio complex on a nearby outcropping [represented on this camping trip by a rather elaborate elf light] and after that by doing crafts.

One day a honeymooning couple from a foreign land picnicked near the Grey Rock River, and hearing fragments of song and smelling fragments of delicious cooking, came on until they found the town of Upper Herrin. They went wild with delight and spent so much money buying Upper Herrin crafts that the only way they were able to dine for the rest of their honeymoon was to sit near other people and ask them if they were going to finish "that," pointing to whatever looked good.

When that couple returned to the place they came from, along with settling down and raising a family (which they did, but which doesn't concern us here, though they did lead interesting lives and their second daughter led an even more interesting life than that), they showed all their friends the things they had bought in Upper Herrin, and told them all how to get there.

After that, Upper Herrin saw a lot of visitors from a lot of foreign lands, and through the eager exchange of crafts for an assortment of currencies, Upper Herrin became more sophisticated and flourished. The pace at last became so hectic that the economy slowed down. After a few years, the hope and effort to revitalize was desperate; and that was when the addition of an historical dimension to Upper Herrin's tourist trade was seen to be effective, and nearly everyone contributed to Upper Herrin's collected history.

Fictions, fireside stories, fantasy, and fact were given equal credit, and the best bits were illustrated. The story of the Antlered Oak Boat of Upper Herrin, suspected to be fantasy, was entirely true. And by a coincidence that would have been as astounding to Upper Herriners as the magical hart had been to their ancestors, this model of the Antlered Oak Boat of Upper Herrin is absolutely accurate, too.

A story like this is also a blessing. A twig-and-pine-cone boat that sails on a stream in the woods (or the popsicle-stick-and-leaf one that sails across the wading pool you set up for your kids) may not need much of a blessing, but it can't hurt! When our elf lights get elaborate (I remember a castle-like one, called the White Towers of Yorre, that I built from pale and shiny rocks, in a little plateau between two gnarled roots of a tree that overhung out campsite) we sometimes tell their stories, and then we can call upon the power of the story to bless the light and the site.

As I sit at the computer, my left brain makes me smile at this thought, but when I'm in the woods under dappled sunlight, breathing the pines' natural incense with the feel of real earth beneath my feet, I know it's true: There are Little People living in the folk tales we tell, as well as in the woods, and when we do them the honor of a story's acknowledgment, they are very generous with their blessings in return.

More than 10 years later, sitting at the computer again, my left brain has a slightly different perspective. These days, as Arizona forests suffer through another year of drought, trees weakened by thirst succumb in record numbers to common bark beetles, and lakes are but memories under landslides that burned woods could not hold back, I believe it's even more important to tell the stories that survive in elf lights and castles and in twig-boats' sailings. Our imaginations, our trusting souls, are real and habitable dimensions, too, and when other environments are devastated, we must keep our hearts hospitable to the magic.

Tools and Accessories

The Sabbats (and to a lesser extent, Esbats) are often more fun to celebrate when a variety of tools and accessories are available. Our Yules, for instance, wouldn't have been nearly so much fun without the cardboard swords the Oak and Holly Kings used to swing; now the battles are enhanced by plastic costume swords with decorated scabbards. A wide and elegant range of accessories are available from many stores and catalogues, but they aren't always within our budgets, and because it just doesn't do to haggle over the cost of ritual accessories, people sometimes need to find other sources.

Check out your local thrift shops. You'll find all kinds of wonderful things in your favorite secondhand stores. The Goddess figure that stood under the North Altar at our first covenstead was a handmade ceramic piece, an eclectic combination of Maiden, Mother, and Crone (and we found Her at Value Village for $1.50). Until She disintegrated and "returned to Herself," we had a straw Maiden from the same thrift shop, and were delighted to see an identical one on a shelf in the Explorer's grade-school library!

I've found tarnished but gorgeous brass and copper chalices at thrift shops, and censers with handles. Candles, sometimes quite overpriced at gift shops, are often sold for just pennies each, and not only tapers, columns, or votives, either. For one Beltane I found a three-sided pink flower candle about 4 inches in diameter. Another time I used a garlanded unicorn candle. (I found both at a thrift shop.) The many discount stores and outlet shops are good places to look, too.

If you want to make God robes (for Samhain, for instance), and you'd like to use real fur without being an environmental bad guy, head to the thrift shop. There you'll find fur coats for pennies on the dollar of their original cost, and you'll be rescuing their spirits when you turn them into ritual robes. The fur that trimmed an antlered headpiece our coven used to use came from a collar I bought for about $2. Now I tend to use fake fur—and even that sometimes turns up in usefully-sized pieces at thrift shops.

Maiden's, Mother's, and Crone's dresses also appear sometimes on thrift shop racks. We've found wonderful shawls and other cape-like wraps (and a couple of real capes, too); on tablecloth racks we've found nice Altar cloths, some handwoven or embroidered. Now and again, something suitable to wrap cards or other Tools shows up. Chosen carefully, hand-washed and consecrated, these things can become a family's or a coven's heirlooms.

Some years ago, I used an old choir robe from the thrift shop when, as part of a presentation, I dressed up as a fairy-tale witch, complete with green-faced mask. After I ran around the assembled listeners, cackling away with my robe a' flying so the audience would recognize the stereotype, I doffed both mask and robe to reveal the real Witch underneath. The old choir robe was easy to get off, and suffered no disrespect even though it got kicked around a little when we danced the spiral later. You could use a similar act at a Halloween party to introduce your children's friends (and yours?) to Wicca, too.

The truth is, I buy virtually all of my clothes at the thrift shop. It saves money, sure, but it's also an act of community and it's a significant form of recycling as well. No matter what I buy at any of the thrift shops I visit, I know I'm helping the planet as well as myself.

Chapter Seven

Passages

We recognize few passages in this culture; coming of age means you can go out to a bar, or a casino. Deep down, most of us expect better. The passage into adulthood is one of the most important we can manage. It's important to humans to get some guidance, feedback, and approval.

Passage rituals reassure us, help us consolidate our confidence and courage to press onward; as life does, as the God/dess does. Celebrating our own passages is part of celebrating the Wheel of the Year, for we are the God: we die and are reborn, and our journey 'round each time is sacred. Passages are to our personal lives what Sabbats are to the Gods.

We—our family, our covens, our Tradition, and Wicca generally—recognize several passages in a life, and we have rituals for most of them. For us, birth, Wiccaning, one or more dedications, and an acknowledgment of puberty pave the way for Initiations. Then, there are Handfastings (and, sometimes, Handpartings), Queenings and Kingings, Cronings and Sagings, and finally, deathing and Requiems.

As our family and coven grew, we added some new passage rites to our Book of Shadows, and we'll probably add more as our practice of the Craft keeps changing. In the meantime, we'll share a few.

Beginnings

Blessing from the East

When I was asked to represent East at the Wiccaning of a friend's baby, here's what I said to the child:

You are latest come among us, but not least,
and in token of your welcome, I bring blessings from the East!

A small crystal affixed to a jewelry pin was bestowed upon the child then, with her father's help, and I said:

May you always think clearly,
may you always trust the Spring.
You will always be loved dearly—
may love always make you sing!
May you always be beginning,
may you always keep the Feasts;
and while the Spiral's spinning,
may you be blesséd by the East.

The Explorer was first dedicated to the Craft when he was seven. He had a "manning" when he was 14 years old; though we had expected to add an initiatory element to his 21st birthday, at his request, it was low-key (dinner and a movie, though as I recall, he had a glass of wine). By that time he no longer considered himself Wiccan, but he understood very clearly that in addition to the legal privileges his maturity gave him, his family and the adults he's known all his life expected him to take more responsibility, too.

At the time that *Family Wicca* first came out, both we and the Explorer anticipated his being Wiccan all his life. We raised him to a Wiccan understanding of the world. If we'd answered his questions with inconsistent nonsense, he'd have noticed and rejected our teachings. If we'd prattled on in meaningless clichés, he'd have stopped paying attention. But we didn't, and though he doesn't call himself a Wiccan now, we still see him living by the Wiccan principles with which he grew up.

Maybe, and I say this with a grin, we taught him too well: He's so grounded in the Wiccan worldview that he doesn't recognize it as distinctively religious! Influenced by the power-grabbing hypocrisy of the spotlighted right-wing fundamentalists, he is suspicious of religions that stand out, and that contradict and disrespect experience. Okay, he doesn't call the Elemental forces by the same names we do, but he is comfortable and sure of himself as part of nature, and he is respectful and appreciative of the rest of life; we can't complain.

Initial Dedication

This was the Explorer's first dedication. It took place in our yard, under the ramada, and before we had planted our circle of grass or laid our adobe bricks. Your own yard, a good friend's yard, a favorite campsite, or the family room will work just as well. We cast a Circle; you'll decide how formally or informally to do a similar dedication for your child/ren.

Begin at dusk. The light should be from candles. Assemble more candles, incense, a white cord, a blue cord, a bowl of warm purified Water, and a box or pouch. The young dedicant is blindfolded and led to the edge of the Circle; there, s/he is asked whether s/he comes to the Circle in perfect love and perfect trust, and (we hope) responds that s/he does.

S/he's then led into the ramada, where his/her hands are washed in the Water. One end of the white cord is tied around his/her waist, and the other end is tied around his/her ankle. S/he is told that before the God/dess, s/he is neither bound nor free.

A sponsor's hand is then placed against the dedicant's chest as the youngster faces North, and the young person is told that s/he is "about to come into a time of special growth and learning. You will come to know more of yourself and the world than you can now imagine. You are about to enter the Circle. Do you have the courage?" S/he replies that s/he does.

All present then lay hands upon the dedicant, and s/he is blessed as follows (by one of the adults present, or by each in turn, or by all in unison): "Blesséd be your feet, that walk upon the Earth. Blesséd be your knees, that kneel at sacred Altars. Blesséd be your potential, that will create life from life. Blesséd be your breasts, formed in strength. Blesséd be your lips, that will learn to speak the sacred words."

The dedicant is then measured with the blue cord, which is knotted at each end to mark his/her height from head to heel. The dedicant's head is measured from one of these knots, and another knot is tied. His/her waist is measured from that knot, and a final knot is tied. The dedicant is then asked if s/he is "ready to pledge your mind to learning, your heart to love, your body to life, your life to peace, and your soul to the Goddess." The knots on the blue cord are then held for the dedicant to kiss in affirmation of the pledge.

Then, with help, the youngster kneels, placing one hand over his/her heart and one on his/her heels, and says: "all between my two hands belongs to the Goddess." Then everyone present, including the dedicant, says "So mote it be!"

The dedicant's blindfold is removed, and the blue cord is handed to him/her, and someone (or everyone) says, "Here is your Measure, to remind you of your promise to learn, love, live fully, work for peace, and respect your Mother Earth." The dedicant accepts the Measure, and places it into the box or pouch s/he's been given. At this time, the white cord is untied and placed in the container, along with the blindfold.

The dedicant's blessed once more, with Water, Crystal, Incense, and Flame, and someone (or everyone) says: "Mother, behold and bless _____, who today joins the circle of Your children." Then everyone present hugs and kisses the dedicant, the Circle's opened, and the feasting begins!

The Explorer's first dedication and the blessing of the East were influenced by Starhawk's rituals. (That's why the cord was blue: the Blue God is the youngest manifestation in Starhawk's descriptions. Were I doing it again, I'd use white or silver now, the colors Campsight assigned to its novices, or the green that Hearth's Gate uses for its dedicants.) Although we no longer use Starhawk's rites, I am still fond of the modifications we made of them. For many years we combined our favorite Starhawkian bits with parts of the Farrars' *A Witches Bible Compleat*. Now we work with original material, which we'll share in another book.

Celebrations

The rituals we've made for the wild sites we love have been some of the most dramatic and powerful we've experienced. These are rites not for our chronological biochemical passages through the physical plane, but for our passages between the Worlds, which we sometimes take for granted.

When we cast our Circles, it is rarely in sheer celebration of being able to step between the Worlds. But this capacity is worth celebrating, and that passage is important. Children of all ages enjoy these rites, too. Younger ones simply immerse themselves in the delight and mystery; older kids can personalize the framework of each such ritual with their own experience.

It helps to be in the woods, away from cynical city walls, where nature's belief in magic can strengthen ours. But what really makes these rituals glow is that they are purely joyful. Sometimes we work on healing, but more often we simply celebrate life. All acts of love and pleasure are Her rituals. Camping makes us feel like being in a huge Circle with the Goddess Herself high priestessing, and it is uniquely refreshing to be part of the rituals the Gods perform.

Often, the only Circle around the ritual we do at camp is the horizon of trees and mountains, for the Guardians do not need to be summoned to their own dwelling places. Sometimes our calling to a place is so strong that it is we who are invoked into the already wholly blessed and sacred sphere.

Campsight has been to southeastern Arizona's Crystal Cave several times. It is one of only three quartz crystal caves in the United States, and though some of the rooms have been stripped by vandals, many of the smaller rooms still glitter in secret. Many a time I have felt, sitting in chambers hardly bigger than geodes, that Merlin was beside me. It's a deep cave; ropes aren't required, but there is genuine risk in there. Entry is relatively easy, and there's a wide shelf where a few people can gather before heading off to explore. We liked to pause and turn our lights off, just to remind ourselves where we were.

Several years ago, this custom inspired to the following ceremony, which is half in modern English and "healf" in Anglo-Saxon. The Anglo-Saxon, being beyond my fonts' capacity to reproduce properly, and difficult for most people to read and pronounce, is written phonetically. If you try reading it out loud, try for a more or less Scandinavian accent to it.

𝔗he 𝔠eremony of the 𝔠rystal 𝔠ave

Onshay thay laikt in oosah yondlickten the shadahelm oosah foryurdan.

The light within us shall illuminate the many darknesses around us.

Onshay oora ferkth yewit ohv thay oon yedollick en thees yedollick clay-ofa, that way may onfee thad tha on-yedollicks whella oosah for-yurdath.

In this finite cosm we embrace the several infinities that surround us.

Onshay oora yelled-yekinnd onspringan frome thees forsainlick cars oonder where way standath, thoor oosah ond frome oosah, toe anbywen tha sickth ohv oora sayfas onh freedness.

Our primal humanity rises from the neglected stones beneath our feet, through us and from us, to clarify the vision of our hearts and minds.

Nima thay strengthoo ohv shadahelm, tha strengthoo ohv sekct ond sailness, ohn way hit habbath mit oosah hereh thees dyeh ond when way gaith frome thees rooma.

We claim the strength of darkness, the strength of peace and silence, and we will have it with us now and when we go from this place.

In tha nahm ohf theh Eortha, befarath en seckt.

In the name of the Earth, go in peace.

Here's another ritual that is magical, too, in more than one way. It's a reunion with our Source, it's about transformation, emotionally and perceptually, and it is open to a child's or an adult's very personal interpretation. Like *The Ceremony of the Crystal Cave*, it both celebrates and facilitates our temporary passages between the Worlds.

Once we held this ceremony beside a stream meandering through a campsite clearing, the clearing filled with 20 or so elf lights. Sitting by the fire afterwards, Canyondancer said it looked like stars had fallen and lay shining on the ground. It was an entirely magical, environmental lullaby for the Explorer, who fell asleep watching the lights twinkle through the window in the tent. You can hold this ceremony or one like it in a wading pool in your yard, or even in the bathtub.

Children of the Water

If you're beside a stream or lake, or even a swimming pool, then use Styrofoam bowls and tall, clear plastic glasses to make candle boats by gluing the glasses into the bowls and setting tea lights in the glasses. If you're working with a wading pool or a small fountain, you can use candles that are made to float. You will also need a chalice filled with your usual ritual drink, and long matches. Purify the "ale," for in this ritual it will be the Water of Life. This ceremony takes place in darkness beside the water; it would be a good idea to purify captive domestic water first.

Silently, the chalice containing the Water of Life is passed. When all have partaken, say in unison, "We are one in the Water of Life. We are One in Life on Earth. We are One."

Exchange private greetings with the water you are standing beside, and when everyone has done this, say in unison, "We are children of the Water; in the Water we are One. From the Water we came to Life; to the Water we come to make our lives whole."

Now light the candles in the boats, and hold them while you say, in unison, "In the flames we come home to the Water; in these lights we offer our dreams to the Water that gave us Life."

Set the candle boats carefully in the water, giving them a gentle push to get them into the current or away from the shore or edge, and say, in unison, "From the Water we came to Life; to the Water we come to make our lives whole. In these lights we are one with the Water. In these lights we are One. We are children of the Water; in the Water we are One."

Pass the chalice once more as you watch the candles drift downstream or bob on the water—and don't forget to pick up the candle boats in the morning.

Some passages occur without any religious or cultural acknowledgment, and when that happens, we are subtly disappointed and demoralized. One gift the Wiccan community is giving to our culture is ritual to mark these passages.

A small group of us (sadly not as close as we used to be) held a Queening ritual one quiet summer weekend, in a wooded area just a couple of hours from Tucson. We got the idea from Budapest's all-in-one *The Holy Book of Women's Mysteries*, (Wingbow Press, 1989) where she described the need to recognize adulthood (not just sexual maturity, but full-blown adulthood), with all its strengths and knowledge.

We decided that a Queening is appropriate for any woman who has achieved her Second Degree and is at least 35 years old, and who has demonstrated her maturity in attitude and deed. Queening conveys no ecclesiastical rank or privilege, but recognizes the practical, secular authority and dignity of the individual woman and the Wiccan context of her life. Speaking of dignity, we happened to find lapel buttons that said YES, YOUR MAJESTY, and we gave those to each other as gifts. We also made "the men" barbecue for us when we came home.

A Queening can be done by a group of women for each other, as ours was, or by friends for one woman. Of course, a Queening can be modified and turned into a Kinging.

Queening

Gathered in a pleasant place, crowns (and any other accouterments, including individual chalices or a single chalice of "mead" for all to share) are arranged to the South, for fullness, maturity, and bright, shining strength. An Altar may be set up, but it should be a simple one.

How you divide up the speeches is up to you; here, lines that should be read by an individual are in *plain Italics*, and lines that should be read by all the Queens together are in ***bold Italics***.

When we were little girls, we dreamed of being Queens. Now we make the dream come true.

Behold, we are women now, and Witches; and the power of the dream is ours.

We are to be crowned Queens, not fearless, but unafraid of fear; not powerful over, but powerful with.

Each now picks up another's crown, and holds it skyward in both hands.

Behold, we take up these crowns in the name of the Triple Goddess and the Horned God.

We accept the beauty and strength of our maturity, and claim our crowns with honor and humility.

Behold, we charge these crowns with the wisdom and courage of trust, and with the power and compassion of love.

Each crowns the woman whose crown she holds, saying as she places the crown,

I complete your Circle as you complete mine.

Behold, these crowns are...

> *...turns of the Spiral.*
> *...arcs of the Cauldron's rim.*
> *...our curving horizons.*

Behold, these crowns are circlets of sisterhood, and behold, we are Queens in the sight of Gods and Witches!

Now the chalice(s) is/are lifted, and the new Queens toast each other. After each Queen has been toasted and the chalice(s) drained, each chalice is held aloft. If a single chalice is used, all have a hand upon it; if individual chalices are used, the bowls are touching.

By the Cauldron of Cerridwen, our lives are changing once again! By love and trust we Queens are bound; in these crowns we find our ground. To change with grace and grow in balance—this we pledge, on crown and chalice!

With harm to none, our will be done. Queens and Priestesses are we: as we will, so mote it be!

Croning and Saging rites might take similar forms; I am pleased to note that now, early in the 21st century, more and more women, many of them not quite Pagan, are creating their own Croning rites. You could even do an "Eldering" ritual for a couple, perhaps on the anniversary of their wedding or handfasting, or of their Initiation or Elevation. The passages, physical and metaphysical, that you mark are yours to choose. (For more suggestions about Passage rites, see *Raising Witches* [New Page Books, 2002].) From birth to death (cradle to womb, you might say) there is much to celebrate, and your life's rituals wait for you to compose them.

A ritual to honor a departed friend can be as simple as lighting a single candle. For other ideas, please see my "death book," *In the Service of Life* (Citadel Press, 2003), or *Eight Sabbats for Witches* (Phoenix Publishing, 1988), by Janet and Stewart Farrar, or *Buckland's Complete Book of Witchcraft* (Llewellyn, 1986). The book composed by Starhawk's group, *The Pagan Book of Living and Dying* (HarperSanFrancisco, 1997), is another good source.

One of Tucson's most respected, experienced, and well-liked priestesses, Delia Morgan, (who has since moved, and is now all those things somewhere else) composed a solitary's Requiem, which we like very much and keep in our Book of Shadows. She graciously gave her permission to include it in *Family Wicca*.

Requiem for a Witch (Delia Morgan, 1990)

Supplies needed:

> Altar with cloth
>
> White taper/pillar candle for Goddess
>
> Water and Salt in dishes
>
> Black taper/pillar candle for the God
>
> Incense and burner
>
> White votive in white container for Deceased
>
> Wand
>
> Vase of flowers
>
> Small bell
>
> Small black stone
>
> 2 to 3 feet of red string/yarn
>
> Rosemary "for remembrance"
>
> Small square of paper
>
> Pen with red ink

Set up the Altar in the North, with flowers at the back, Goddess image and candle on the left, Horned God image and candle on the right. Arrange other items so as to leave a large space in the middle of the Altar. Purify Water, bless Salt, and mix a pinch of Salt into Water.

Light the white candle and say, "Oh, Great Mother Goddess, who gives birth to all that is."

Light the black candle and say, "Oh, Great Horned God, Lord of death and the Summerland."

Light the incense and say, "I ask that you be with me tonight and bless this rite."

Turn deosil in a complete circle and say, "Oh, Mighty Ones of the four Quarters—Air and Fire and Water and Earth—I ask that you attend and empower this rite. Blesséd be."

(It is optional at this point to cast and purify a Circle, purifying yourself with oil, and so on.) Say, "Hear ye that _____, a friend and sister/brother in the Craft, has passed beyond the veil."

Ring the bell three times slowly and pause. Say, "Tonight I remember her/him and honor her/his spirit as I bid her/him farewell."

Lay the red string in a spiral on the Altar. Say, "S/he travels now upon the Great Spiral of death and rebirth. Infinite and eternal is the cord which binds us to the Mother Goddess. Night leads to dawn, winter to spring; endless is the Spirit's journey, and ever the Circle shall turn."

Light the votive candle and place it in the middle of the Spiral, and say, "May your spirit be rekindled in new flesh; may you arise in peace."

Lay the black stone to one side of the votive. Say, "I bid you farewell on your journey through the Shadows. May you find peace and rest in the Summerland."

Lay rosemary to the other side of the votive. Say, "You will be remembered in the hearts and minds of those who love you."

Holding the votive candle, circle three times around widdershins to symbolize the journey to the Underworld. Replace the candle in the Spiral.

Face West. Say, "You have passed the Western Gateways and set sail upon dark Waters. Fear not, for the Horned One will lead you to the Summerland, and back to the Cauldron of Cerridwen, to be born again of the Great Mother."

Turn deosil to each of the four Quarters, starting in the West. (West symbolizes dusk, autumn, endings, and the Gateway to the

Underworld.) Sprinkle salt water to the West. Say, "By the Waters that are Her womb, may you be reborn in love."

Sprinkle salt to the North. Say, "By the Earth that is Her body, may you be reborn in strength."

Wave incense to the East. Say, "By the Air that is Her breath, may you be reborn in joy."

Raise the votive candle to the South, saying, "By the Fire that is Her spirit, may your light shine brightly in a new and even better life."

Holding the votive candle, circle three times deosil for rebirth, ending at North. Replace the votive in the Spiral. Say, "Blesséd be, _____."

Draw an invoking pentagram above the votive with your wand or finger. Say, "You are a child of the Goddess, and if it be your wish, may you be reborn into the Family of Wicca."

Now sit by the Altar for a while, remembering your friend, his or her best qualities, your time together. If you feel comfortable doing so, talk to your friend's spirit, saying how you feel.

Take the piece of paper and write or draw on it some expressions of your feelings or wishes for him or her: initials, runes, hearts, pentagram, moons, happy face; whatever feels right. Place the paper under the votive candle.

When your contemplation is finished, you can bless some wine and raise a toast to your friend, or sing some fitting songs (*We All Come from the Goddess, Hoof and Horn*, and so on). When you have done this, face the Altar. Say, "Great Mother Goddess, Great Horned God, and ye Mighty Ones of the four Quarters, thank you for attending this rite."

Ring the bell three times and say, "This rite is now ended, but may the loving energies continue to follow and bless _____ on his/her journey. So mote it be."

(If a Circle has been formally cast, it should now be formally opened.) Blow out the Altar candles but let the votive continue to burn all the way down, or burn it for several consecutive nights until it is completely gone.

Later, gather the rosemary, black stone, and paper talisman, and wrap them with the red string. Bury them together in the ground where they will not be disturbed. They can be put in the grave if there is one; it's an ancient widespread Pagan custom to bury "gifts" with the dead to help them on their journey.

Bless a chalice of wine and hold it above the burial (of the rosemary, stone, and talisman) site. Say, "Bless éd is the Great Mother, who gives life to the universe. From Her we all proceed, and unto Her we must all return. She is the Ground of Being that dwells within us, changeless, boundless and eternal, and Her love is poured out upon the Earth." Pour the wine out upon the earth, and lay flowers on the top. Say, "Bless éd be."

We add to this ritual's "grave goods" symbols of the deceased's treasures—scraps of food (a feast of the deceased favorite's is nice afterwards), ribbons, a key, bits of cloth from well-worn clothes, a curl of hair if that's possible. Everything should be blessed before being with or for the deceased.

Several years ago, when a great-grandmother died, I wrote a song for her. Subsequently, I've written a couple more "death songs;" here's one of them. If you like, you can use it as it is; or feel free to change a few words to make it more specific and appropriate in your own circumstances. It lends itself very well to harmony.

(A) Summerland Lullaby

Music and lyrics by
Ashleen O'Gaea

Transcribed by
Katharina Lau

I will sing you that I love you, I will sing you that I'm glad we met; I will sing you that it's time to say good-bye. I will sing you that I'll miss you. I will sing you that I won't for-get. Close your eyes and I will sing you a Sum-mer-land lul-la bye. O-ver there the sunlight lingers and the grass is wet with dew. O-ver there the God will bring us where the Summer's always new. O-ver here the sto-ry's ending, o-ver there it's just be - gun. O-ver here the Moon is waning, o-ver there you'll have the Sun.

Second Verse

I hear the God's bells ringing
to call you over there,
and soon you will be singing
with the sunlight on your hair.

Over here the story's ending,
over there it starts anew…
and we who are remaining
know God/dess loves you as we do.

Alternate

In our hearts your mem'ry's glowing;
we still hold our love for you.
Over there your new life's growing
and the Gods will make you new.

Chapter Eight

Living Mythically

In his (still) popular books and (occasionally replayed on cable and available on VHS or DVD) television series, Joseph Campbell advised "living mythically." We find this consistent with Wicca, and appropriate to family life. Of course it doesn't mean dressing in sandals and brandishing swords (well, maybe at Yule and Litha), or setting out on vacation with no map or compass! So what *does* "living mythically" mean to a modern Wiccan family?

We interpret it to mean living life as an adventure. That sounds obvious. But how do you make an adventure out of making a bed or changing a diaper, or any other mundane chore?

Nothing is wrong with imagining the aisle between the couch and wall as a strait fraught with monsters that can only be defeated with the vacuum cleaner, or the floor under the kitchen table to be the lair of a beast against which the only effective protection is a mop. Nor is there anything the matter with offering yourself rewards: when you and Vinegar and Water have vanquished those Perilous Windows, you can feast upon cookies and tea!

It is profoundly true that the most important thing in any adventurer's life is Home—the hearth and hearts for which the adventure is undertaken in the first place. Whether you're safe at table in your clan's Great Hall, or sitting with companions around a fire at the mouth of a cave, there is still dinner to provide and share, literally and figuratively.

Heroes, heras, and bards of old put a good deal of themselves into every meal they prepared. There was the hunt (or the gather or scavenge), the building of the fire, the care for the fire and the turning of the spit, and the intimate relationship with the Gods and spirits to be guarded as well. A mistake in dealing with any of these resulted in no evening meal at best, and an imperiled quest at worst!

Most of us don't have to hunt or gather food from the wild now (although some supermarkets make a good approximation). Most of us can kindle and coax our cooking fires with a flick of the wrist. But we must still groom our relationships with the Gods and spirits; we must not forget the God's willing death that serves life in the harvest of grain and game, or the Goddess' love that grows us all, season by season, life by life, year after year.

Like adventurers of old, we must guard our hearths wisely, but not harshly. It is no less true for us than it was for the wandering heroes and queens of old that the stranger who begs succor could be a Wise One. Neglecting to share what we have is still at least a rejection of opportunity.

The magical tools these strangers bestow in exchange for our hospitality are more subtle these days. No more (well, not as often, anyway) the talking harp, the righteous sword, the ever-full pouch. But how full of healing is the heart that loves unconditionally? How fortunate is the long-forgotten favor finally returned, greater than it was granted or remembered? How much magic is in the courage of stopping to help the fallen when the path most easily taken avoids them?

Mystery is everywhere. Not just the mystery of what the driver ahead of us is going to do, either, but real mystery, with spine-tingling potential.

Endless possibilities often do not suit the bureaucracies in which we live—not the institutional bureaucracies, and not our family bureaucracies. We've all learned a protective insensitivity. If we want to live mythically, we have to resensitize and re-orient ourselves in the widening world we are just rediscovering.

Almost all the cultural prejudice against Wiccan customs derives from the propaganda strategies used to conquer Pagans when various patriarchal empires were expanding. Even a few of the Ten Commandments (never mind The Rules today) seem ideally suited to suppression of Goddess-worshiping cultures. Most of the prejudices against Paganism encountered now are based on the uninformed observations and interpretations of foreign invaders, like the Romans, who measured every culture against their own and found most others wanting. (You may have noticed your neighbor taking the same attitude!) By patriarchal and increasingly monotheistic standards, it became impossible to accept European Pagans as civilized; by those same standards, it's impossible for some people now to accept Wiccans as civilized.

Much as science fiction movies present alien worlds one dimensionally (with extras all having the same clothes and the same hair cut, and doing the same things, without schools, hospitals, grocery stores, or parks, and only the main characters showing any hint of being well-rounded), our records of our religious ancestors' lives are conveniently biased toward the reporting conquerors' "superiority."

Sociologists today write about the age-old technique of dehumanizing the enemy to rationalize the torture, slaughter, and enslavement of civilians. We are just beginning to loosen our grip on modern prejudices against the Germans and the Japanese, defeated more than 50 years ago and much changed since then. (Since Bush the Lesser's war in Iraq, we've renewed our prejudice against the Germans, and the French too. Here we go again!) We have barely begun to reform our prejudices against Witches, even though Paganism fell victim to the same propaganda techniques much longer ago.

As adventurers, this is what we face: an ignorant, frightened wilderness that just happens to be where we were born. Understanding it in this context, we don't have to take our families' (or society's or the fundies') anger and confusion personally. Many of us had to overcome a cultural aversion to the word "witch," and for some of us this was difficult despite the Goddess' motivation. It's not going to be any easier for people who've spent their whole life following, nay, virtually worshiping, The Rules.

The rules by which many of us and most of our parents were raised are, according to John Bradshaw (with whom we heartily agree), abusive rules. Spare the rod, spoil the child, that sort of thing. Fit in, hide your feelings; the pain is *supposed* to be tremendous. Once we understand that, though, and realize that the Goddess asks *naught* of sacrifice in that sense, we can erase those tapes so they don't play back in our minds whenever we're under stress.

Then, rather than responding defensively to questions, skepticism, disinterest, ridicule, accusation, and so on, we can discover the root fear and address it gently, as we'd approach a wounded animal. We don't guarantee this approach will be successful if your only goal is to change someone's mind, but a loving approach leaves our consciences clean, and is healing for everyone concerned.

Sometimes the root fears are easy to calm. Several years ago, my mom heard some self-styled "witch" say on *The Tonight Show* that she celebrated the Summer's Solstice by dancing naked around a bonfire and burning money. Justifiably perplexed, Mom called and asked if that was what we did. Nope, I said, and we had a good giggle about wishing we had money to burn.

Sometimes the fears are harder to identify and assuage. Magic and meditation are both useful tools with which to control ourselves in difficult situations. If a family member is seriously aggressive or offensive, binding may help; but beware, for as you bind, so are you bound, and even the most carefully considered and worded binding spell is probably manipulative. We prefer spells along these lines:

Let the Goddess speak through me
that my meaning they may clearly see.

Show me the words that I can say
so I may be understood today.

Resolving conflicts in family relationships is one of the most difficult healings or quests any of us undertake. The obstacles are many. Family is a realm in which it is prudent to take Campbell's advice to "live mythically," and to remember to "follow your bliss" and answer your own callings, too.

We should not be any less prepared for our adventures across the landscape of family relationships than we are for any other adventure; it is not a less-mythic quest. In fact, the myths from which our rites and spectacles are drawn are, broadly, about each generation's place-taking in the world family, and about conflict resolution.

Realizing that, you can see that it just doesn't get any more mythical than family. Before every foray, we need to ground and center, collect and meditate with our tools, remember our purpose, and bless ourselves. When you take this trouble, not only are visits with family less stressful, but you are also setting good examples for your children.

We all hope to avoid making any major mistakes in bringing up our children. We all hope that when our kids are our age, their core relationships (with us!) will be solid and affirmative, not draining or anxious. But we all know that they will encounter adventures in their lives, adventures on which we won't accompany them, though we hope to hear about those when next we gather together in the Great Hall (whether that's at Gramma's or in the Summerland). The examples we show our children, the constancy with which we keep our vows to enter Circles in perfect love and perfect trust, are among the Tools they will use when they take up their own quests.

Years ago, when *Close Encounters of the Third Kind* was a new movie, and we still liked to see new movies in theaters, Canyondancer and I were so taken with the film that for the next few months, whenever we saw clouds like the ones in the movie, we drove up to the foothills and...waited. The spaceships haven't come yet, and my left brain does not imagine they ever will.

Indeed, my left brain is deeply offended by suggestions that the work of ancient civilizations—Egyptian temples and pyramids, Stonehenge, North and South American mounds and cities—were engineered by aliens! I confess to being sternly intolerant of assertions that my ancestors were feeble of mind and body and spirit. As for the notion that giant figures fully visible only from the air must have been landing strips, I reject it, and take these for religious artifacts, geometric community offerings to the Gods. (And the guys who made the crop circles have confessed, so we can stop squawking about aliens making those, too.)

My right brain is less political, and trusts not only that aliens might one day stop by for a cup of tea, but also that they would be wise and gentle people (who would admire our ancestors' building prowess). Both my brains agree that any culture cooperative enough, and with time, energy, and resources for inter-planetary travel will have overcome voluntary aggression and be on peaceful missions of sociable exploration.

Those are the only bounds my right brain knows. Apart from trusting—knowing—that the nature of life is peaceful (behold, She is the Mother of all things, and Her love is poured forth across the universe, and love unto all beings is Her law), there's no limit to my belief in possibilities.

Trust in this limitlessness is mythic. Before the Goddess, we are neither bound nor free, and as above, so below; the universe is neither bound nor free (something physics concludes, too). There are laws we must follow, of course, but they are not laws we can violate and be punished for breaking. They are laws that we cannot break, like the laws of three-dimensional existence. It's not a question of risking jail time for living six-dimensionally, after all.

Nor are the natural consequences of certain behaviors (broken bones for walking off the edge of a cliff, for instance) punishments. Rain from clouds is not a punishment, it just is. We can explain it in terms of the laws of physics that science has articulated for us, and these laws apply everywhere. They do not depend on "good" or "bad" behavior.

And yet we must choose to believe, choose to make it true, if we want to live mythically, that everything happens "for a reason." We need to know the places of our lives well enough to recognize their similarities, well enough to see their patterns. We need to understand all the Worlds as part of the same cosmic psycho-biosphere. We need to see Signs and Portents everywhere, and know that what we do matters in the World, and to the World, because what we see and do *is* the World.

Physics offers an example. Watch your hand move through the air, and you can tell its speed and direction. But if you look at it from the corner of your eye, you can tell either which way or how fast it's moving—your perspective doesn't allow you to be accurate about both. If you wave your hand around behind your head, where you can't see it at all, it could be going anywhere, at any speed. Studying micro-micro particles in photo-tanks, physicists find the same limitations—and they agree that until a particle's velocity or direction is measured, it could be going anywhere, at any speed.

Consider the example of J.R.R. Tolkien to help make this clear, if it is not already so. Tolkien's *The Hobbit* and *The Lord of the Rings* trilogy have meant many things to many people. Some have taken the work to be an allegory about World War II. In an undergraduate thesis, I asserted that Bilbo's and Frodo's adventures, and the natural laws they followed, offered proof of Tolkien's own religious dogma, though the population of Middle Earth never referred to its gods or its faith. Tolkien himself insisted (like Freud?) that it was "just a story" for the kids.

But Tolkien (a Christian), like many Wiccans, was steeped in histories of all kinds (political, social, linguistic, and mythic), and whether he was conscious of it or not, this opened his mind to the cosmic adventure. His books would never have been so popular if they *had* been just about world war, or just a proof of religious logic. It was only because they weren't "just" allegory or proof that they could be allegory and proof, *too*.

Until we choose to see something (an event or circumstance, a person, a relationship) in a certain way, we have the potential to see it in an almost infinite number of ways. Perspective, visual or psycho-spiritual, is a matter of choice, and that is the practical as well as theoretical truth of most situations. Is vacuuming a dull chore, or a way of banking the fire for the long, magical night? Is changing a diaper something to rush through holding your breath (okay, sometimes it is), or brave camaraderie? Without a flexible perception to allow her to recognize magic in mundane disguise, how far can any hera follow her quest?

In our experience, the best way to live mythically is to *choose* to live mythically, to put even the mundane tasks into a wider perspective. I make an effort to respect cows, for they are sacred to Cerridwen, yet I do not want to live like a cow, unable to cross the metal bars on the road and unable to distinguish between real barriers and painted ones.

Society paints a lot of barriers on the road, many of them derived from patriarchal monotheistic systems (the other PMS). On the Wiccan quest to restore the Goddess' Altars, literally and figuratively, that magical flexibility of perception is both our most important tool and the hardest to win. For all of us, an important part of living mythically is testing the barriers. Are they real, or are they only paint? And if they are real, are they really impassable? Earth, Air, Fire, Water, and Spirit. No paint. Respect the Goddess' boundaries, which are few and subtle; consider all the painted ones blasphemies or tests, and approach them accordingly.

The Explorer learned this early, and learned it well, and yes, sometimes it caused trouble. We told him (among other things) that he never had to accept brute force for legitimate authority. So, he eventually tangled with a teacher who believed that the most important lesson a student can learn is to do what s/he's told without question. Confronted with this (blasphemy? test?) we said that we would rather come to a 100 parent-teacher conferences than raise the Explorer to an other-directed manhood.

Of course, there are compromises to make. Sometimes a hero has to play along with giants or monsters in order to escape them, or to earn the magical tools in their keeping. Sometimes a kid has to be still and do what the teacher says, whether it makes any sense or not. Sometimes adults have to be still and do what the boss says, whether it makes any sense or not. But let's be flexible about that, too. Sometimes things make more sense when considered in a wider context. In school, for example, some kids may need to go over the lesson one more time, and the ones who already understand don't need to feel put-upon when the teacher goes through it again to keep everybody caught up.

Nevertheless, learning how and when to compromise is a useful skill for any adventurer. The corollary is knowing when (and how) to stand unmoved by intimidation, to be undeceived by manipulation. Legitimate (creative, win-win) compromise must take place within a framework of nonnegotiable and clearly defined standards and values. Even if you can't meet your standards all the time, the efforts you make to meet them strengthen you, your children, and your community.

You don't (at least not often) set out on a quest without knowing either your objective or the signs to recognize it. Your kid's childhood is a long night around the fire when the shaman (that's you) teaches the signs, describes the quests. If your own shaman (your parents, Catholic school, and so on) was an imposter, then you'll have to find a real one, or be your own, and get the signs straight before you go on. A family and/or a coven is a great hearth around which to gather for this.

The effort made to distinguish your standards from those by which you can be oppressed is equally, if not more, important. Your family will need to define its values in terms of your own Wiccan Tradition. Because the God/dess speaks many languages, you might not put things the same way we do, but all Wiccans need to address the same basic issues. Here's our conceptual framework:

> ► An ye harm none, do as ye will. Love unto all beings is Her law. What you give to the world, the world will give back to you threefold. This holds for attitudes, too: as you will, so mote it be.

> ► You shall be free from slavery. This requires emotional honesty and some political attention so you notice whether or not you're being enslaved.

> ► We'll be around again, so we like to keep it nice (the Earth, the political system, etc.). It's similar to cleaning up before you go on vacation, so you can relax in a clean house when you get home. (It's good to have a lasagna, literally or figurative, in the freezer when you get back, too.)

> ► When nature compels us, it's toward survival and creativity, toward babies, and works of art and peace. If what you're doing gets in the way of survival or creativity, it needs to be re-evaluated. We have choices; that's evolutionary, too. Creatures with our cerebral capacity for choice are unlikely to evolve in an environment that offers no choices, just as the opposable thumb wouldn't have evolved if there were nothing for us to hold with our improved grasp. Brown moths don't turn white if there are no light-barked trees on which to hide.

> ► The universe is friendly. On his deathbed, Einstein reportedly said that "Is the universe friendly?" is the only important question. Perhaps he heard the Goddess, for his answer was

that it is, and that's Her answer, too. Life is complementary, not adversarial. This implies that teamwork is natural. We don't give up any individuality when we contribute our individual talents to the team (the coven, the community, the world, and so on). Neither do we give anything up when we become one with the Goddess. In either case, we don't fade away to make room for the Big Thing, we expand until we are the Big Thing.

▶ We are naturally empowered. This is both a religious and a generational conviction. Idealism is a function of the conceptual cortex, which is one of our evolutionary specialities. It's biochemical, and we think that's wonderful because it implies that peace and love and trust are biochemical.

Paleoanthropologists have given ample evidence that, while we're capable of it, violence isn't "our nature," it's a defense mechanism. We have created a world in which we live in constant need of defense! The systems by which we've organized our local and global life put us at emotional and material war everywhere. We are crowded like once gentle, now aggressive rats in a cage, reacting the same way to the same stimuli. As much energy as you can relieve from anxiety can be used to enjoy life, and to work more powerful magic to help free your quest-companions, members of your immediate family, Iraqis, or endangered trees or beasts. ("Iraqis" were among the examples I mentioned in the first edition; the more things change, the more things stay the same.)

Wicca is one of the few Western religions that considers brain chemistry sacred and gives you control over it in ritual. Talk about power to the people! You *are* God/dess; big responsibility; big satisfaction in accepting it. When you live in harmony with the Goddess, you find that you are living in harmony with each other and with yourself, too, for you are God/dess.

You are God/dess. The rainforest is God/dess. Your husband or wife is God/dess. Your children are God/dess. The neighbors, even the mean or reclusive ones, are God/dess. The fundies are God/dess. People you don't like are God/dess. People who scare you are God/dess. (My Tradition holds that our religious obligation, as Wiccans, is to find out how everyone and everything else is God/dess, and find a way to appreciate the sacred in all things. My Tradition does not hold that it has to be easy to meet this obligation.)

I've been asked if we believe that pets have souls. Yes. (And yes, our pets are God/dess.) When I first wrote this book, I noted that our youngest cat channeled the Goddess' Queen of Hel aspect. I'd like to note now that after harassing two older cats to death, this cat grew old and died, in my arms, and is buried in our yard. The Explorer, though denying a belief in classic reincarnation, cautioned us, when we went to the Humane Society for new kitties, to make sure the ones we chose were born before Mikey died, so we'd know she wasn't back in one of them. They were, and she wasn't, and our current cats, Milo, Hal, and Bette Noire, are the best and most delightful we've ever known.

Families are God/dess, too, or can be, in Wicca. In this book, we've shared with you some of the ways that our family life is Wiccan. Some of these ways your family may already know, and some we hope you'll come to know as fondly as we do. We hope, too, that your family will become more aware of its own traditions, the old ones, and the ones yet to be.

Are they ordinary cats? Maybe they're faery cats, or gods in disguise, or magical creatures with powers to bestow! At the least, they're blessings and maybe even tests of our powers—patience in particular?

In our growing understanding of God/dess, our family is still growing (even though the Explorer's grown now and lives on his own), as you and yours will. And in the God/dess' love, we now bid you farewell; go in peace! Merry part, and merry meet again. Blesséd be!

Glossary

ADF: Arn Draiocht Fein (arn ree-oct fain): a Druid Fellowship. North America's largest tradition of Neo-Pagan Druidry.

adobe: (uh-DOE-bee) A mixture of dirt, straw, and water shaped into bricks and dried in the sun. Modern adobe bricks are made according to the ancient formula and stabilized (invisibly) with asphalt so they won't disintegrate in the weather. Bricks are about 16 inches long, 8 inches wide, and 4 inches thick.

Anglo-Saxon: Old English, spoken from the fifth through the 11th centuries. Several cognates remain in modern English, many of them in popular use; it's not your French you should be excusing! One source of the word "witch" is the Anglo-Saxon "wic," which means "to bend or shape." (Chaucer's language, by the way, was Middle English; Arthur and Robin Hood might have heard, or even spoken, Anglo-Saxon.)

as above, so below: A Wiccan way of saying that natural laws apply universally and that our interconnectedness makes all realms metaphors for one another.

astral: A name for the planes or dimensions of reality existing beyond ordinary sight and measurement. Some are personal and some are universal.

athame: (uh-THA-may; ATHA-may) A ritual knife, usually but not always double-edged, used to cast Circles and for other magical purposes; never used as a physical weapon.

Beltane: May Day. One of the two most significant Wiccan Sabbats. The traditional Maypole braided with ribbons represents the creative union (sacred marriage, *heiros gamos*) of the Goddess and God and the many ways Their fertility is manifest in our lives. There are several spellings.

besom: (BESS-um) The brushy part of a broom, the bristles; the whole broom.

between the Worlds: Wccans know the physical world is not the only world in which we live, that there are other realms and dimensions, including the Underworld, the Spirit World, and many other aspects of the astral, emotional, and psychological planes. When we worship in a Circle, we are in a sacred space where the physical and the potential interface, where all times and dimensions meet, and where our rites and magic can draw upon their combined energies. We call this place (and other places that feel that way to us) "between the Worlds."

beyond the Veil: Beyond what we can see, hear, taste, touch, or know intellectually. Ghosts and the vastness of the universe are among those things that exist beyond the Veil. When we say that the Veil is thin, we mean it's easier to access and appreciate those things that are normally hidden from us behind the Veil.

birthmother (birthfather; birthparents): The biological mother, who actually gives birth to a baby, whether she will raise the child herself or adopt the baby out to other parents. (The biological father; the biological parents, whether or not they are a couple, whether or not they plan to share parenting responsibilities.)

bolline: (boe-LEEN) White-handled knife used for ritual cutting of cakes, cords, herbs, and so on. The blade is often crescent-shaped; it's never used as a material weapon.

Book of Shadows: The handwritten book of rituals, spells, charms, chants, journal entries, meditations, songs, poems, dreams, and so on, kept by most Witches. Traditionally black-covered, the "B.O.S." is generally not shown to the uninitiated. These days many of us have formal Books and working Books, which are often loose-leaf; some of us even have Disks of Shadows.

Brigid: (BRIJ-id or breed) One of the Goddess' names, and a Sabbat also known as Bride (breed) or Imbolc; non-Wiccans may call it Candlemas. Celebrated on the first or second of February, this Sabbat marks the beginning of Spring, and honors the Mother Goddess' recovery from the God's rebirth at Yule, and honors the God's growth, which is by now visible in first sprouts and slightly longer days.

Bride: (breed) See **Brigid**.

bound nor unbound/free: At initiation, a Witch is said to be "neither bound nor free" in relationship with the God/dess. This is because s/he is bound by natural laws, which are impossible to break.

censer: A covered incense burner that can be carried around the Circle during ritual.

Charge of the Goddess: One of the best-loved pieces of Wiccan liturgical material, composed by Doreen Valiente for Gerald Gardner. Adapted by many

Traditions of the Craft, the *Charge* is instruction, direction, description, encouragement, promise, and mystery. See also Appendix A.

Cauldron-luck: What else would you call a pot-luck for Witches? When the Tucson Area Wiccan-Pagan Network began to meet monthly in a public park so interested newcomers could meet and break bread together, we wanted people to know we had a sense of humor, so we coined the term.

charm: Dramatic or material, a charm combines writing, speaking, and/or drawing with herbs and elemental symbols and calls upon/contains their power, directing it toward a goal like protection, health, or good fortune.

Circle: A ritually dedicated space where Wiccans' rites are conducted "between the Worlds." Marked at least by psychic energy and the priestess' sword or athame, the circumference also supports Quarter candles at the compass points. Once cast, a Circle may not be entered or left until a Door, quickly resealed, is ritually cut. The psychic energy of a Circle is usually grounded at the close of ritual, but the physical demarcations may be left in place.

consensus decision-making: Listening to and caring about everybody's needs, expectations, ideas, concerns, and objections before deciding any question. You still have to compromise, but your cooperation is acknowledged and everybody's needs, if not preferences, are met in pursuit of a common goal. (See Starhawk's *Truth or Dare*.)

Cords of Life: Mabon activity we adapted from Starhawk's ritual; three to four-foot lengths of cord braided and decorated with seed pods, feathers, twigs, shells, beads, and so on, to represent your personal harvest.

coven: (CUV-en) A Wiccan congregation, traditionally, six couples and a leader; now, usually from three to 13 Wiccans. Covens may be affiliated with specific Wiccan Traditions, or eclectic.

covenstead: The home of a coven, where it usually meets; usually but not always the home of the coven leader.

cowan: (COW-un) Not Wiccan; not Neo-Pagan. An archaic term, really, but I like it.

crone: A menopausal or post-menopausal Wiccan. The time at which a woman assumes her cronehood is intensely individual. Because our culture is unkind to age, we can be uncomfortable with its wisdom; the crone is not yet fully appreciated, but as Boomers age, she will be.

croning: A ritual to recognize and announce a woman's attainment of cronehood; a celebration of her accomplishments, her depth, her value, her potential, and her perspective. Happily, cowan women are conducting cronings, too.

Cross-quarters: The Solstices and Equinoxes mark the Quarters of the Year; the other four Sabbats (Bride, Beltane, Lammas, and Samhain) are the Cross-quarters.

death in the service of life: Natural or willing death that contributes to the life of the group (tribe, species, planet, and so on). Death in childbirth, rescue, defense of culture, that sort of thing (in the wild, predation, aging, and seed cycles, for example). *In the Service of Life: a Wiccan Perspective on Death* (Citadel Press, 2003) is the title of O'Gaea's third book.

deathing: Sitting with a dying person and performing rituals to make his or her death easier. By ritual or improvisation, preparing someone for and guiding them through their death experience.

Dedication: A rite preliminary to Initiation. Appropriate for young or beginning students not yet ready for First Degree but prepared to make an initial commitment to further study and practice of Wicca.

Degrees: Recognition of levels of study and experience in a Tradition of the Craft. Most Trads that use a Degree system recognize three Degrees; very generally, a First Degree knows the basics and is competent to participate in most rites; a Second Degree is authorized to teach and may organize and lead a coven under supervision; a Third Degree is fully ordained. Degrees are authorized and given by a Wiccan's own High Priest/ess, who is a personal witness to the Initiate's qualifications. We've come to believe that Degrees beyond First should not be taken by people who don't intend to make a life-long commitment to functioning as fully ordained clergy.

deosil: Clockwise; the usual direction of movement in and around a Circle. (The other way is called "widdershins.")

desire, end of all: In this context, "desire" is the basic set of mortal needs and senses by which we're aware of being separate from our Mother. The end of it occurs when in death (or shamanistic experience) our consciousness expands beyond discrete individuality to Wholeness, a.k.a. returning to the Goddess.

elf lights: Illuminated candle-cairns welcoming the local Little People to the decorated site.

Esbats: Full or new Moon gatherings. Magic is generally done at Esbats rather than at Sabbats. Esbats focus on the Goddess, one of Whose symbols is the Moon.

evil: Wicca does not "believe in" evil in the sense that monotheisms do; we think of it as an adjective rather than as a noun. We tend to ascribe horrifically unacceptable behavior to fear, ignorance, or brain damage. When we use the word, we're usually talking about seriously bad vibes.

five-fold kiss: The source of our "blesséd be," the five-fold kiss is usually part of an Initiation. It's a blessing given with kisses and the following words, which vary slightly among Traditions:

> *Blesséd be...thy feet, which walk the sacred paths*
> *...thy knees, that kneel at sacred Altars*

...thy sex, without which we would not be

...thy breasts, formed in strength and beauty

...thy lips, that speak the names of the Gods

fundamentalist (fundy, fundies): A politically right-wing religious conservative (extreme) who believes that the whole and only truth about life, the universe, and everything is contained in the Christian Bible. Often aggressively evangelical, not interested in other people's perspectives, and not much concerned with other people's Constitutional rights.

Gaian: Of Gaia, of the Earth; referring to the fact that the Earth is a living organism of which all living things, inert features, and natural operating systems are a part.

Gates, the: Metaphorical reference to the passage from the mundane world to other realms, or from life to death: upon death, a person passes "through the Gates." In a near-death experience or life-changing crisis, one can face the Guardian at the Gates. Druids "open the Gates" in ritual, similarly to the way Wiccans go between the Worlds.

God, the: A personification of aspects of life's energy, the Wiccan symbol of "all that dies and is reborn." The Sun is one of His forms/symbols. He is often depicted with horns or antlers to represent the game that falls to the hunt so the tribe may live. He is also seen as the Green Man, representing the grain and other plants that die in the annual harvest so that life can go on. Born from the womb of Mother Earth at Yule, He mates with the Goddess at Beltane, enjoys His prime through the Summer, willingly dies in Fall's harvest, and rules the Underworld from Samhain till Yule. He is also represented by the Oak (Summer) and Holly (Winter) Kings. The Sabbats are celebrated in honor of His life's cycle.

Goddess, the: A personification of aspects of life's energy, the Wiccan symbol of "all that is eternal and generative." She is the principle by and through which death becomes life again. Mother Earth, Mother Nature. Maiden, Mother, Crone. Her awareness is the source of our humanity; we are the vehicle of Her awareness. (See also **thealogy** and Appendix A.)

grave goods: A symbolic and magical collection of memorabilia, gifts, and supplies for someone who has died; a pouch, box, or packet of ritual credentials and Tools for the spirit world. The goods themselves are buried or cremated with the deceased; it is their psychic energy that will equip the journeying soul.

Great Rite: The *heiros gamos*, or sacred marriage, of the Goddess and the God. Enacted ritually, it takes one of several forms, most commonly as a blessing of the ritual wine or ale (the priestess lowers her athame into a chalice held by the priest). On special occasions the Great Rite may be performed literally—

215

in which case privately; not to be confused with Hollywood images of Pagan orgies, which are not a part of Wiccan worship.

ground and center: Collect yourself, focus on the ritual at hand, clear your mind of mundane distractions and concerns so your energy will be strong. Find the quiet center. Often achieved through meditation and/or visualization.

Guardians (of the Watchtowers): Elemental energies whose images combine the corresponding characteristics of the Directions they symbolize. The Guardians of the Watchtowers are invoked as the Circle is cast to add elemental and directional strengths, protections, and inspirations to the proceedings. (See Appendix B.)

guided meditations: Read aloud or played on a tape, a narration of an astral journey through self-awareness, or to a specific astral site to explore memory and other personal realms, or to meet with other souls or spirits to find or exchange information or work together. Used to discover alternative attitudes toward problems and issues, sometimes to change behavior, and to effect light trance states for relaxation and healing.

Handfasting: A Wiccan wedding. A Handfasting can bind a couple in matrimony for a year and a day, after which they may decide whether to part or Handfast permanently, or, if the officiating priest/esses are authorized in their state, it may be a legal wedding.

hera: (HAIR-uh, HERE-uh) A female protagonist on a mythic quest or adventure, literary or literal.

hero: (HE-roe) A male protagonist on a mythic quest or adventure, literary or literal.

Holly King: Anglo-Celtic image of one of a pair of archetypical twins, Holly is the King of the Waning Year, who wins the duel at the Summer's Solstice; his brother Oak wins at the Winter's Solstice to preside over the Waxing Year. Their myth survives not only in Wiccan ritual, but in folk literature, where Cock Robin's exploits conjure the older story; Light and Dark twins are basic characters in most mythic cycles.

HP: (aiche-PEE) Abbreviation for High Priest.

HPs: (aiche-pee-ESS) Abbreviation for High Priestess.

HPMS: (AICHE-pee-em-ess) An HP or HPs whose behavior is too high-falutin'. It's not a term in wide use, but here in Tucson we used to use it fairly often. It's a good thing that we don't need it much now—but it's still needed often enough that I'm including it here. (This term and its use mean no offense to women afflicted with PMS, premenstrual syndrome, which is a difficult, and often painful to the point of debilitation, medical syndrome not to be made light of.)

Initiation: Ordination in the Craft, usually to one of three Degrees. Most Traditions recognize self-initiation to First Degree. Many Trads recognize all Degrees from other Trads, but coven-specific initiations are still the norm. Second and Third Degrees are given/meaningful only in the context of a coven and/or community. An initiation is symbolic of a mythic quest, death and rebirth, and must be requested by a student or apprentice; it is not granted unless the HP/s is satisfied with the student's work or progress. Self-initiation is less formal, but requires an equal commitment.

Kinging: A ritual recognizing and announcing a man's achievement of full maturity. For men who are beyond youth but not yet old enough to be Sages. Kinging is unique to Wicca (as far as we know) but does not confer a clerical degree. (See also Queening.)

Lammas: (LOMM-uss) The Cross-quarter Sabbat between Litha and Mabon, also called Lughnassad. Celebrating the first of the Year's three harvest festivals on August second, Lammas is traditionally observed with cornbread and strawberries. The Sabbat's name comes from the Anglo-Saxon for "loaf mass."

Litha: (LEE-ha) Mid-Summer. The Summer's Solstice, when the Sun begins to wane. As in Shakespeare, a night of magic and delight. A celebration of the prime of [the God's] life—the abundance of growth, the health of the herds and crops, the good weather—in full awareness of mortality and that Winter is on its way.

Little People: The indigenous spirits and legendary occupants of a given land, and/or the ancestors of a given culture.

livestone: Stones, stone articles, or crystals still inhabited by the benevolent spirit of the source stone (boulder, mountain, outcropping, and so on).

livewood: Twigs, branches, or wooden articles still inhabited by the benevolent spirit (Dryad) of the parent tree. Dryads can project clones of themselves into beads, staffs, wands, and so on, if they are properly asked when the wood is collected.

Lughnassad(h): (LOO-na-sadh; loo-NASS-adh) See **Lammas**; the name "Lughnassad" comes from harvest games that the God Lugh established in His [foster] mother's honor.

Mabon: (MAY-bon, muh-BON) The Autumn Equinox, second of three harvest festivals. Mabon sees feasting to celebrate the success of the harvest, even while the Goddess mourns the death of Her Son and Lover in the fallen grain. A good time to remember your local food bank.

magic: Nonordinary activity or experience; affecting change in accordance with intention/will. You can work magic, you can witness magic, you can feel it around or nearby. It ranges in "size and shape" from love to ritual, from personal to local (or regional or global), from human to Gaian. It can be large or small, and while it certainly includes the candle, cord, rune, and other magic we do in our Circles, it's not just that. In its broadest sense, magic is anything that amazes or delights you, answers a need beyond ordinary meeting, or makes you "cry for happy." Yes, there is "bad magic," magic that is coercive and manipulative, but Wiccans avoid it, and creative, growthful magic is much stronger, and much, much more common.

Moons: See **Esbats**.

mundane: Something performed or perceived as unmagical, ordinary, everyday, material, practical, secular. The 9-to-5 rat race, rent, and PTA routine and its attendant concerns. "Muggle stuff," we can say now that everyone knows Harry Potter.

nitwitchery: Occasional or habitual inconsiderate behavior among Wiccans and other Pagans, which risks insult or injury to other Wiccans or Pagans. Showing off. Loudly, publically or otherwise obnoxiously violating common etiquette. Self-aggrandizing exploitation of Craft knowledge or practice. (The term was, as far as we know, coined by an HPs in Tucson.) (See **HPMS**.)

nonordinary: Out of the ordinary, following apparently different and often intuitive rules. Magical. Nonordinary reality is not entirely subjective. (See also **astral**.)

Oak King: Anglo-Celtic image of one of the archetypical twins of Light and Dark. Oak is the King of the Waxing Year who is victorious in the duel at the Winter's Solstice; Holly is the King of the Waning Year who wins the Battle at Mid-Summer. Gawain and the Green Knight is one story about the Kings' Battle. (See also **Holly King**.)

other-directed: Motivated mostly or entirely by other people's standards and expectations and/or needs, or by assumptions about other people's standards, expectations, and/or needs. People who are often convince themselves that those standards, expectations, and needs are really their own, or they accept that other people know what's best for them.

occult: (oh-CULT, sometimes AH-cult) It means "hidden." You know those "hidden pictures" puzzles they make for kids? And those 3-D books that you hold in front of you and suddenly from geometric designs, roses, and swans pop out? It's like that.

Pagan: It comes from the Latin word "pagani," which means country-dweller. It means non-Christian because country-dwellers were the last to be converted. We capitalize it because we capitalize Lutheran and Christian. It's an umbrella term that describes a number of specific religions as well as a general nonmonotheism.

passages: Significant transitions. Biological (birthdays, hormones), geographical, emotional, social, political, etc., especially when archetypical and universal. Any transition or aspect of transition that is important to the person in transit.

Families, covens, neighborhoods, governments, societies, and planets go through phases and transitions, too, and it's appropriate to mark those passages as well.

patriarchal: Any social, economic, religious, or other system or institution, concept, or principle that's organized around or derived from the consideration of partners and children as property. We call it patriarchy because it developed after we figured out fatherhood; and individuals (females as well) can also be patriarchal. Patriarchal systems aren't always terrible, but they have been overused and abused in the last few hundred years.

perfect love and perfect trust: An idea, a goal, a metaphor, and expression of feeling safe as a part of nature; an attitude we choose to take. It doesn't mean gullibility, it means not assuming some right to get mad or even, even if it's in your face. (See Appendix C.)

PMS, the other: Patriarchal Monotheistic System(s)

Quarter-calls: Invocations, sometimes rhyming, to the Quarters, or Directional powers (see **Guardians of the Watchtowers**). Calling Quarters is one important step in casting a Circle, part of preparing it before invoking the God/dess. Also referred to as just plain "Calls."

Queening: A ritual recognizing and announcing a woman's achievement of full maturity. For women who are beyond youth but not yet old enough to be Crones. Queening is unique to Wicca (as far as we know) but does not confer a clerical degree. (See also **Kinging**.)

raising energy: Increasing the energy level in a group for the purpose of directing and releasing that energy toward an agreed-upon goal or target. Methods include breathing in unison, chanting, dancing, and variations of those activities.

ramada: A Southwestern-style covered patio, a roof supported by poles; there may or may not be sides. In Spanish the word means "arbor," natural or built.

Rede, the Wiccan: "An ye harm none, do as ye will." Witches pay more attention to harming none than to doing anything; and the none we harm is all of life. "Will," by the way, means your deepest calling, your purpose-for-several-lives, not just what you want.

reincarnation: Recycling for souls. People have different ideas about how it works and who comes back as what, but Witches accept it because nature obviously recycles all energy, including ours. (We think it's likely that reincarnation works in several ways, because most everything else in Nature does.)

ritual: Choreographed and/or scripted worship; structured religious behavior which may or may not be premeditated. Wiccan ritual generally begins with using various forms of the four Elements to cast a Circle, into which the Goddess and God are invited as witnesses or participants. The purpose of ritual is usually celebration and/or magic. Ritual ranges from standard liturgical material and form to reverent personal habit.

rockeries: Rock gardens or arrangements, natural or hand built.

Rules, the: From *Making Sense of the Sixties,* a PBS documentary: Obey authority, conceal your feelings, fit in with the group, and don't even *think* about sex.

Rune, the Witches': A chant used to raise power, usually recited while walking or running a circle around an Altar or within sacred space. The version we use is modified by memory from the Farrars' *Witches Bible Compleat* (Magickal Child Publishing, 1984):

> *Darksome night and shining Moon*
> *East then South then West then North*
> *Harken to the Witches' Rune*
> *For here I come to call you forth!*
> *Earth and Water, Air and Fire*
> *Wand and pentacle and sword*
> *Work you all to my desire*
> *Hark you all unto my word!*
> *Cords and censer, scourge and knife,*
> *Powers of the Witches' blade,*
> *Wake you all now unto life,*
> *Come now, as the charm is made*
> *Queen of Heaven, Queen of Hel,*
> *Hornéd Hunter of the night,*
> *Lend Your power unto my spell,*
> *Work my will by magic rite!*
> *By all the power of Land and Sea,*
> *By all the might of Moon and Sun,*
> *As I do will, so mote it be!*
> *Chant the spell and **be it DONE!***

Runes: Ancient alphabets used today for ritual and magic. (For more about their magical meanings and use, see Freya Aswynn's *Northern Mysteries & Magick* (Llewellyn Publications, 1951).) Witches use a variety of Runic alphabets, some of which are relatively new.

Sabbats: Solar holidays marking the Sun's course and the God's life through the Year. The Solstices and Equinoxes are the Lesser Sabbats; the Greater Sabbats are Bride, Beltane, Lammas, and Samhain, also known as the Cross-quarters.

Sage: An elder Wiccan man, a male crone.

Saging: (SAGE-ing) A ritual to recognize and announce a man's attainment of sagehood; a celebration of his accomplishments, his depth, his value, his potential, and his perspective.

Samhain: (SOW-wun, SAH-wayne) From Gaelic words meaning "end of Summer." The Witches' new year, the last of three harvest festivals, and a family reunion including the spirits of our belovéd dead, celebrated on October 31st or November 1st. With Beltane one of the two most significant Sabbats on the Wiccan liturgical calendar.

SCA: The Society for Creative Anachronism.

sealing a spell: Closing your work on a spell with a word or gesture to contain the energy you've put into it. Can be elaborate or simple.

S/self: With a capital S, the Wholeness of which we are all a part, a reference to the Goddess aspect of your personality; with a small s, that part of you conscious of being an individual.

shamanic or shamanistic: States of consciousness and explorations of the astral realms to which those states of consciousness are gateways. Involving nonordinary perception, experience, or activity.

Sight: The "second sight," clairvoyance; awareness of other dimensions and their inhabitants. May also refer to related "second senses," like "having a feeling" or "just knowing."

skyclad: Without robes; "clad in the sky;" physically naked for ritual.

sound energy: Atonal chanting; energy raised by wordless sound, "aaah," "ohhhh," and so on, to release and direct energy toward a goal. Energy rises with the pitch and/or volume and is released with a shout, or with sudden silence.

spell: A direction of power, often rhyming, spoken over a symbol of the event or circumstance to be influenced. Also, a symbolic act (such as writing a Rune, drawing a design, lighting a candle, and so on) to direct energy to influence an event or situation.

'stead: See **covenstead** and/or **Traditionstead**.

story blessings or spells: Stories from or about ancestral and other non-ordinary realms, told to direct power from those realms into ordinary life. Often spontaneous, and often seeming to come from natural objects with which the storyteller's interacting.

Summerland: Where Wiccans and Druids say we go when we die; an astral "place" where our souls rest between incarnations. It encompasses the Underworld, Fairyland, and other realms, several astral planes, and a variety of states of mind and being. Also known by the Irish names of Tir na Nog and the Land of Youth.

Suns: See **Sabbats**

taboo: It means "forbidden" in our culture (and in this book), but in its original context can refer to an obligation as well as a prohibition.

tapes: The soundtracks of our parents' voices, or those of other people who influenced us early on, repeating rules, observations, and criticisms. All the "you should" and "you're just" and "why can't you?" stuff we heard between birth and leaving home. Self-psychology involves erasing and rerecording the tapes; so does study for Initiation.

thealogy: The study of Goddess and the relationships between Goddess and humanity; study of Wiccan and some other Pagan beliefs, philosophies, and worldviews. Similar to "theology," but having to do with a generative principle that is feminine rather than masculine.

Threefold Law, the: The understanding that "what you put into the world comes back to you threefold." It's on a par with the laws of physics in that it's a natural characteristic of life rather than imposed upon us by any supernatural being or institution. It works in any/all dimensions.

together hug: A group hug. We say "together hug" when it's personal and intimate, like at home before bed, and "group hug" when it's more public, like at a picnic or after a coven ritual.

Traditions: (also called **Trads**) Sects of Wicca: Seax, Gardnerian, Dianic, Alexandrian, Adventure, Feri, Family, Eclectic, and so on. We capitalize it to distinguish our religious denominations from small-t traditions, which are customs.

Traditionstead: (also called **Trad-stead**) Home base or headquarters of a Tradition, usually home of the founder(s) while s/he or they are alive.

usual way: (of casting a Circle) Most people interested in Wicca have been taught, found in a book, or developed their own way of casting a Circle, which includes calling and releasing the Quarters, invoking and thanking the Gods, and conducting Cakes and Ale. I refer those who don't have a "usual way," to Appendix A in *Celebrating the Seasons of Life*: *Samhain to Ostara* (New Page Books, 2004).

Vine God: A representation of the foliate God, a figure twisted from vines and dried in time for Lammas (or maybe another harvest festival). We fill ours with foil-wrapped cornbread so when the Vine God "dies" in the bonfire, the bread that's made from the grain He represents is left to feed us.

visualization: Seeing something in your mind's eye, whether your physical eyes are open or closed.

Watchtowers: See **Guardians of the Watchtowers**.

Wheel of the Year: Wicca's liturgical calendar; a conceptualization of the solar year, marked by the eight Sabbats which represent the stages of the God's life, death, and rebirth. Shows the relationship of the seasons to Wiccan holidays.

widdershins: Counterclockwise. This direction of movement is sometimes taken to undraw the Circle, but rarely otherwise. (The other direction is deosil.)

Wicca: A modern form of the ancient religious tradition of Paleo-European cultures. Heavily-armed monotheism conquered Europe's formal Pagan religions; after an absence of about 600 years, the ancient perspective were reinterpreted and rearticulated in the 18th and 19th centuries by the Romantic Movement. Wicca was named and developed in the mid-20th century by Gerald Gardner and his colleagues. Wicca's beliefs are in a **Goddess** and **God** representing natural forces and relationships, and include the notion that the Web of Life is holy, that humanity's natural state is in harmony with the rest of life, that there's plenty of ignorance and fear and some chemical imbalance, but no organized, sentient presence of evil, that this world and the Otherworld (see **Summerland**) are equally real and important, that psychic and paranormal experience are natural, that **reincarnation** is a universal principle, and that **magic** is a natural force.

Wiccan Scripture: Nature. Everything from watching the squirrels bury nuts in the park to astrophysics—natural history and how it happens. Also, some pieces of liturgical material, like the **Charge of the Goddess** (see Appendix A) along with the **Rede** and the **Threefold Law**. Wicca has no ultimate book of authority, but each Tradition has a Book of Shadows, and so do most individual Wiccans.

Weber bonfire: A biggish ritual fire in the barbecue or grill, in the absence of any other suitable fire ring, pit, or place.

Wiccaning: A ritual blessing babies born into the Wiccan community, introducing them to the Guardians and the God/dess, and promising care and support for the child as s/he grows.

Wise Ones: Ancestral elders, heras, heroes, Guardians, aspects of the God/dess, elemental Spirits, Little People, and so on. Archetypical personifications of wisdom and experience.

Worlds, between the: See **between the Worlds**.

Witch: *Not* a euphemism for "bitch," the word comes from the Anglo-Saxon *wicce* and *wicca*, which were pronounced *wee-cheh* and *wee-chah*, feminine and masculine respectively. One of the root meanings is "bend or shape," and Witches are the ones who do the bending and shaping. Over the centuries, as the language has changed, the two words have telescoped to one and the pronunciation has changed. The modern word refers to both men and women. We capitalize it when we're referring to someone who considers any denomination of Witchcraft their religion, but not when it's used in a sociological sense. For more information about this, see Isaac Bonewits' *Witchcraft: a Concise Guide* (Earth Religion Press, 2001).

Witchcraft: Often but not always a synonym for Wicca, Witchcraft is really a wider category into which Wicca fits. All Wiccans are Witches, but not all Witches are Wiccans.

wonder child: A Jungian term naming that part of our awareness that experiences the world as an amazing, wonderful, mythic place to explore. That aspect of ourselves that works magic; our reservoir of perfect love and perfect trust. The part of us that appreciates gestalts, symbolic perception, "starlight vision," and lateral thinking.

younger self: Starhawk's designation for the wonder child. She calls its complement the "talking self." "Inner child" is Bradshaw's term for this part of ourselves.

Yule: The Winter's Solstice, when the Sun is reborn from the Womb of the Earth. (See also **Oak King** and **Holly King**, **Wheel of the Year**, **Sabbats**, and **the God.**)

Appendix A

The Charge of the Goddess

A few years ago, on our first trip to England, I had the great privilege of meeting with one of the Craft's original priestesses, who was kind enough to tell me that she liked *The Family Wicca Book*, but why, she asked, had I seen fit to change the way Doreen Valiente had written the *Charge*? Mrs. Crowther thought this was a bit presumptuous, and I do see her point. On the other hand, I've heard that Ms. Valiente never wanted the *Charge* to be memorized and recited, but offered it as an example of inspiration, and meant it as encouragement to allow ourselves to be similarly inspired.

The Goddess does speak to us individually, or at least we all hear Her uniquely. Although I cannot deny that the original version of the *Charge* is wonderful and inspiring and deeply meaningful, I must also acknowledge that my experience—in life and in the Craft—is different than Doreen Valiente's was. She came from a different generation, and a different culture, and a different Tradition of Wicca. She pitched her tent in the base camp, and mine's set up in another place. So yes, for myself and for the Adventure Tradition that's developed from Campsight's work,

I modified the *Charge*, and my modified version is what this Appendix is about. I don't apologize for it; but I don't mean any disrespect by it, either.

Perhaps I should also add that we don't use the *Charge* in ritual very often. I refer to it often, and think of it as a guideline, a working rule, same as I understand the Rede and the Law, more than I recite it in Circle.

Listen to the words of the Great Mother, Who of old was known as Artemis, Astarte, Isis, Cerridwen, Diana, Melusine, Brigid, and by many other names:

Whenever you have need of anything, once in the month— and better it be when the Moon is full—you shall assemble in some sacred place, there to adore the Spirit of Me, Who is queen of all the Witches; you who would learn magic, but have not yet gained its deepest secrets, there will I teach you. And you shall be free from slavery, and in token that you are truly free, you shall be naked in your rites.

Sing! Feast! Dance! Make music and love, all in My presence, for Mine is the spirit of ecstacy, and Mine as well is joy on Earth, and love unto all beings is My law. Mine is the secret Door that opens upon youth; mine is the Cup of the wine of life, that is, the Cauldron of Cerridwen that is the holy Grail of immortality. On Earth, I give knowledge of the Spirit eternal, and beyond death, I give peace, and freedom, and reunion with those who have gone before.

Nor do I ask aught of sacrifice, for behold: I am the Mother of all things, and My love is poured forth across the Lands.

Now hear the words of the Star Goddess, the dust of Whose heels is the host of heaven, Whose body encircles the universe:

I, Who am the beauty of the green Earth, and the white Moon among the stars, the Mysteries of the waters and the Desire in all hearts, I call upon your souls to arise and come unto Me, for I am the soul of nature that gives life to the universe. From Me all things proceed, and unto Me all things return.

Let my worship be in the heart that rejoices, for behold: all acts of love and pleasure are My rituals. Let there be beauty and strength, power and compassion, honor and humility, and mirth and reverence with you ... and you who seek to know Me, know that all your seeking and yearning shall be to no avail, unless you shall know the Mystery: that if that which you seek you do not find within, you shall surely never find it without. For behold: I have been with you since the beginning, and I am that which is attained at the end of all desire.

This is the version of the *Charge of the Goddess* that guides Campsight's and Adventure's work under the full Moon, and our understanding of the world and our interpretation of what happens in it. With the Threefold Law (that the energy you put into the world comes back to you "three-fold") and the Wiccan Rede ("an ye harm none, do as ye will"), the *Charge* directs us to live in the Goddess and according to Her will, in harmony with nature and with respect and deference for the life that's been here longer than we have. (Like most Pagans, we try to learn from our elders, not annihilate them.)

Because Wicca is not dogma-dependent, we can't just tell our kids to memorize a set of rules. We have to help our children experience the world as we know it to be. Not all of today's Wiccan parents were brought up in the Craft, so we can't all fall back on memories of growing up Wiccan when we wonder how to raise our kids. The *Charge* and other liturgical pieces are our sources, our collective memory.

We must value experience highly enough to give it to our kids, so that the *Charge* is an illumination and not the experience itself. But how do you translate these beautiful words into experience? By beginning with the basics, and forging a family lifestyle that reflects your own interpretation!

According to Webster, a "charge" is laid upon us with authority: we are obligated by it. The question is, what is our obligation and how can we fulfill it? Some of our understandings follow; your family will build its own traditions of inquiry and interpretation as you ask yourselves what the *Charge* means to you.

> ► With our needs, we are to assemble to adore Her. To do this, we must be aware of our needs, something not as simple as it sounds in this day and age. To be aware of your needs requires the joint effort of both sides of your brain, knowing and feeling. (Don't listen to what the commercials say you need.)

> ► It is best, but not exclusively permissible, to assemble when the Moon is full. But many of us meet at the new Moon, and some of us meet at the quarter Moons as well. Assembling once a month (at least) is a clear direction, though.

> ► When we meet, we adore She who is our queen, and She teaches us magic. We meet to learn magic whenever we have need of anything, from which we may fairly conclude that magic will help us supply our needs. (We may also take "learn" to have more than one meaning. We can learn *at* the Moon how to work magic, and we can also learn that it works— according to the Rede and the Law, of course.)

> ► The Goddess promises and commands that we shall be free from slavery, and that in token of this freedom we are to be naked in our rites. There are many forms of slavery, and many ways to be naked, just as there are many Traditions of Wicca. Our nakedness, physical and/or emotional, is a token, a symbol

of our freedom from slavery; our nakedness needs to be appropriate to the slaveries we overcome. If you grew up with a lousy body image, then physical nakedness may be appropriate (or an appropriate goal). If you grew up protecting family lies, then baring feelings and family secrets might be a more meaningful nakedness.

We can raise our children to be comfortable with physical and emotional nakedness—honesty, love, and trust—and they can be free from all slaveries. Don't forget, though, that grandparents and the local Child Protective Services may take a different view of skyclad working, and wear robes in the Circles your children attend. (When we can't meet skyclad, for being in public or with children, many of us are barefoot, symbolizing nakedness and putting ourselves in direct contact with the ground. On the other hand, at some Moons in the forest, Campsighters have been skyclad *except* for hiking boots—and yes, that looks as funny as you think it does.)

▶ We are commanded to sing and feast and dance, and make music and love, all in the Goddess' presence. You can (many of us do) interpret that to mean that we must do these things in every Circle. Chants are quite often our songs, Cakes and Ale comprise a feast, our movement around the Circle is dancing (if we use bells, there's more music). And making love? Blessing the Ale is a symbolic version of the Great Rite, and in Circle, symbolic is real. I'd also like to remind you that cooing at a baby, romping with the dog or cat, laughing with friends, and other such activities are also forms of love-making.

You can also take it to mean that whenever we are doing any of these things, singing, feasting, dancing, or making love, we are invoking the Goddess. Indeed, in the second half of the *Charge*, She asks us to "behold," to witness, that "all acts of love and pleasure" are Her rituals. Hers is the spirit of ecstacy, so when we are ecstatic, we manifest Her. Hers as well is joy on Earth, so when we create and experience joy, we invoke and manifest the Goddess.

➤ Love unto all beings is Her law, and to follow it, we must find Her love within ourselves and let it guide us all the time, not just when we're in formal Circles. She has told us to be naked in our rites, but the *Charge* does not limit the occasions on which we're to sing, feast, dance, and so on, or show love unto all beings. These are, in fact, things we need to do in every aspect of our lives.

➤ She does not ask us to sacrifice to Her, for Her love is poured forth across the Lands. We take this to mean that the natural cycles of life and death keep the energy flowing as it should, and that no additional sacrifices—no death that is not in the service of life—is either required or accepted. This cycle (birth, growth, death, and rebirth) operates in every realm (planes, Lands, dimensions, Worlds) and their constancy, expressed succinctly in the phrase "as above, so below," is the one, the whole, the substance and manifestation of Her love.

➤ Her authority to call upon our souls to arise and come to Her is that She is the life-giving soul of nature. From Her we come, and unto Her we shall return. In between, we are the Goddess in mind and molecule, for it was Her joy that created us all. You and I and all our kids are made of this joy, and to prove it, our bodies are 97 percent the waters of Her womb.

➤ In worship of Her, we are to rejoice; and all our acts of love and pleasure, from the brush of your cheek against the baby's to the time you give to your community, from sex to a great meal, are Her rituals.

▶ "Let there be beauty and strength, power and compassion, honor and humility, and mirth and reverence with you." This is one of the most meaningful elements of the *Charge*, and it tells us very clearly that these qualities are not opposites. Our social structure presumes that they are, that these qualities paired in the *Charge* don't "go together." The *Charge* not only affirms for us that these qualities are complements, it obligates us to integrate them into our attitudes and behaviors.

So, what we find in the *Charge* is that the world is not as the patriarchs describe it. The truth about the world is not fully revealed in the *Charge*, for ours is a religion of experience. But the *Charge* outlines the perspectives we must take to experience the Goddess' truth. From this we can derive certain fundamentals about life, the universe, and everything.

First, we must be aware of our needs. Starhawk has developed this idea, summing it up in the quoted advice to follow the self to find the Self. But because we are all related in the Goddess, to be fully aware of our needs we must also be meaningfully aware of other' needs and cycles, including the planet's. We must make ourselves comfortable with magic, too, for magic is one Tool with which we can meet our needs.

We must be naked (which means undisguised as well as unrobed) in our rites, and we must be free from slavery. Freedom from slavery requires recognition of enslavement. Freedom from slavery is also a precondition of nakedness, because you can't be sure you're naked if you don't know what you look like, and you can't know what you look like if other people define your life.

Facing these issues and exploring them honestly and thoroughly, resolving them with an awareness of the standards we hold (individually and as families and covens), and being satisfied with the source and substance of our standards—that's how we're all charged by the Goddess.

Love, in fact, is Her law: act lovingly toward all beings. Are mountains beings? Mineral deposits? Forests? Rivers? Oceans? Lava fields?

Deserts? The atmosphere? Bugs? You don't have to agree in your interpretations with me or anybody else. You do have to make your own interpretations, and take responsibility for them.

Keep beauty, strength, power, compassion, honor, humility, mirth, and reverence with you, and remember that these qualities are not mutually exclusive. From this and the Goddess' rejection of sacrifice, be assured that life is not a vale of suffering, and pain is not your lot. It may be an accompaniment, but it's not your purpose.

Something else to notice about the *Charge* is that it does not contain any "Thou shalt nots." You don't need to be restrained by threat or prohibition. You come from the Goddess, who is beauty and joy and mystery. Your life is not offensive to Her, and your pleasures on Earth are not illusory distractions from a separate spiritual reality. She does not hide from you, but invites you to experience Her mystery and learn Her magic. She does not require aught of sacrifice, and She will not punish you when you die. Beyond death, She gives peace and freedom, and reunion with those who have gone before.

This is a very different understanding of human nature and the world than monotheistic traditions give. You're not shameful slime with slim hopes of attaining grace, nor is the world a vile, expendable stage upon which a cosmic battle between supernatural "good" and "evil" rages. (Nor is it illusory.)

Your life looks very different when you see it from the Goddess' perspective, which She shares in the *Charge*. That perspective has been withheld from you—from all of us—for a long time, and reconstructing it for yourself and your children is an enormous task, one that is enormously worthwhile. And remember, if that which you seek you do not find within, you shall surely not find it in any book.

Appendix B

Correspondences

Direction	East	South	West	North
Colors	white, blue yellow	red, gold orange	blue, green aqua	brown, black green
Tools	staff, wand athame	sword cauldron	chalice cauldron	pentacle bowl
Element	Air	Fire	Water	Earth
Time	sunrise, morning	noon	dusk afternoon	night midnight
Season	Spring	Summer	Autumn	Winter
Guardians	Zephyrs	Salamanders	Merpeople	Dwarves
Attributes	thought imagination inspiration	activity passion consummation	emotion intuition	physical strength death and rebirth

This is not an exhaustive table of correspondences; there's no such thing! Most books about Wicca [including my two volumes of *Celebrating the Seasons of Life* (New Page Books, 2004)] contain a chart like this, according to particular Traditions and in varying degrees of detail. This one is meant to give you an idea of the sorts of correspondences Wicca makes among directions, colors, times of day, elements, and so forth. Because this is a book for your family, this table is a simple one, suitable for Wiccans of almost any age. As your family and your practice of Wicca grows, you should add correspondences of greater complexity and personal significance to this brief list; and when you see lists in other books, make notes about the correspondences that make sense to you.

Among Wiccans, there are differences of opinion about correspondences. One of the most significant is the association of certain Tools to the Directions. Some people put the sword and athame in the East, because the blades are sharp, cutting edges to make distinctions (making distinctions is a function of the mind, and of vision, which are commonly associated with East and Air).

These people usually put the wand and the staff in the South, because those tools are often made of wood, which has a rather well-known association with Fire, which is associated with the South. But others put the wand and the staff in the East, for they are conjuring tools, and conjuration has its root in vision and imagination. For these folks, the athame and the sword are associated with South, for these metal tools are forged in Fire. Every Tradition has some unique associations; your family will have some, too. What matters is that the correspondences you use make sense to you, and that you use them consistently in your work (otherwise, they have no power at all).

But *why* correspondences? Well, why coordinate a wardrobe? You feel better dressed, more powerful, and more credible, when your clothes go together, when you're not wearing a raggedy sweatshirt with tuxedo pants or a satin skirt, or orange and brown plaid with aqua checks.

You're more effective in the world when what you wear complements your body and your purpose (that's why you probably wear nicer clothes to work or to dinner with somebody special than you do to wash the car or clean the basement).

In the same way, most of us find that our magic works better when all the things we use to work it are coordinated to the same purpose. Are you doing magic to sleep better? Use nighttime colors and do the ritual at night. If you're doing money magic, do it when the Moon is waxing, because that's what you want your income to do. Again, what matters is that the correspondences you use make sense to you, and that you use them consistently in your work; otherwise, they have no power at all, just like the most wonderful outfit will look goofy on you if you're not comfortable wearing it.

Appendix C

Perfect Love and Perfect Trust

In the first edition of *Family Wicca*, Appendix C was a list of catalogue sources. Some of those listed are out of business now, and the others have Web sites (and many of you reading this book are more skillful at surfing the Internet than I am). In forms that can't be updated regularly, it's always risky to print names and addresses of "sources," so this edition of *Family Wicca* is not "going there." On the other hand, I hear a lot of confusion about "perfect love and perfect trust," and love and trust are so relevant to family life that I want to take a closer look at these Wiccan passwords.

As you may know, "perfect love and perfect trust" are the passwords most Traditions want to hear from a dedicant entering an Initiation Circle. The idea in that context is that if you don't love Wicca and the Gods and yourself unconditionally, and fully trust the people who are initiating you, you ought to turn back. But what about the rest of the time? How does this "perfect love and perfect trust" stuff work in other Circles, and in mundane life?

A number of us have been (or feel) betrayed by other Wiccans, people we once loved and trusted, and with whom we now don't ever want to circle again. "I won't be in a Circle of any size with someone I can't love and don't trust," is how most of us put it. I've talked about this with several well-taught and experienced Wiccans, and I have to tell you that my take on it seems to be unusual. If my impression about that is correct, then I'm happy to share it with you, because you're probably already familiar with the more common perspective.

We talk about the Goddess' unconditional love, and by that we generally mean that She loves us no matter what kind of mistakes we make. That doesn't means She loves us *for* making mistakes. Nor does it mean that She doesn't expect us to take responsibility for them, and make up for them when we can, and learn from them even when there's nothing we can do to make up for them.

In the same way, we might "love" some people even though they have disappointed or betrayed us. But what kind of love is that? We use the phrase "perfect love," but we don't usually define it. Not too long ago, though, I read a book called *In the Spirit of Happiness* (Back Bay Books, 2001) which I don't think does use the phrase, but nevertheless defines "perfect love" pretty well. The book was written by the (Greek Orthodox) Monks of New Skete. And they talk about love as wanting what is best for the other person.

Sometimes, what's best for the other person isn't "good" for us. If someone breaks faith with me, I can perhaps find comfort in the thought that s/he will, somehow, grow from that experience. But I'm not responsible for or in charge of the consequences that person faces for anything s/he does; I'm responsible for the consequences of my behavior. From my perspective, perfect love is genuinely wanting (intending, really) the best outcome, short- and long-term, for that person in these circumstances. Am I entitled to be angry? Probably. Am I allowed to stomp my foot and hope s/he feels bad about hurting me? Probably. As long as that's venting my immediate feeling, and does not become the attitude I choose to maintain.

Why is it important to desire and intend the best for other people, even if (especially if) they hurt us inadvertently or deliberately? It's important because one of our beliefs (as expressed in our interpretation of the Wiccan Rede) is that we can all achieve our true wills without interfering with anyone else's. This suggests that even when other people hurt us, we can find a way to be who we're meant to be, and to complete our cosmic quests. In that context, we don't need to seek revenge; indeed, that would be us getting in our own way!

Does this mean we shouldn't press charges when that's appropriate in the civil or criminal realm? No, it doesn't. Perfect love—desiring and intending "the best" for others—may mean listening patiently instead of rolling our eyes and looking for an escape from a tedious conversation, but it doesn't mean excusing wrongdoing. It's loving to listen for something interesting in what we assume will be a boring chat, and it's loving to hope that a person finds opportunities for growth in the natural or social or legal consequences of his or her behavior. It's not loving to favor your own convenience over someone else's feelings, and it's not loving to dismiss an offender's needs with the thought that "s/he had it coming."

When we decide that we can't love somebody (can't intend and desire the best for them) then indeed we should not circle with that person. But it's not because their energy will inhibit the Circle, it's because our attitude will be disruptive! It's not anybody else's responsibility to be easy to love; it's ours to control our own energies.

Another point that the monks make in *Happiness* is that love isn't a feeling, it's an act of will. I had to think about that idea long and hard when I read it, and I still stop and consider it periodically. The more I explore that idea, the better I like it. We do have a choice about our intent, and to desire the best for others, whether or not what's best for them is best for us, is most certainly an intention, an act of will. And isn't being aware of our will, and choosing to act in accordance with it, one of the spiritual skills Wicca teaches us to develop? I think it is!

In our lives, we can follow the Goddess' example in many ways. There are lots of kinds of love, ranging from the "love" that, according to Starhawk, the particles of atoms have for each other, the love that keeps the universe physically together, to the "love" that romantic couples have for each other; there are many other loves of which we can partake, too. Perhaps most basic is the love we have of other people simply because they are, like us, Earthlings. Does loving people in this sense (respecting their humanity—or, if we take it beyond humanity, respecting their "organism-ity" and their fundamental right to live) mean we have to *like* everybody?

Certainly not! I respect the rest of life, and as a Wiccan probably count more in that category, like mountains and ocean- or wind-current systems, than some people do. But I still kill the ant that chews on my toe, or the kissing bug wandering across the living room floor. (Actually, as I revise this edition, I have a rather painfully swollen and rashy kissing bug bite on my ankle!) I don't like centipedes or earwigs, I'm not particularly fond of okra or fascists, and there are certain people, even here in my home community, that I'd rather not be in the same room with if I can help it. There are some people with whom I wouldn't circle in an intimate setting, and people I won't ever invite to my home. But, unlike some of my friends, I won't absent myself from a large public Circle just because people on my short list are in it.

In the context of love being an act of will, a choice to desire and intend the best for others, I think that "perfect" love is the best you can do at any given moment. If you can acknowledge another person's humanity, even while you rail about their flaws, that's love enough. Have you never been bullheaded yourself? (Ooh, a God-image used to mean stubborn and frustrating: that tells us something, eh?) And is the Goddess not still there when you've got sense enough to seek Her again?

As for "perfect" trust: well if someone has "messed with you," then you know just how far you can trust them, and once you know that, they can't "mess" with you anymore. You can trust them to do what they think is in their best interest, or to do what they know how to do, and no, I'm not being sarcastic. When it comes to trust, we aren't supposed to *not* have to pay attention.

There are a couple of people of my near acquaintance who "get to me." More often than I would like to, I find myself annoyed with something one or the other of them has said or done. I sometimes mutter as if it were their fault I'm ticked off about those things. Sometimes, indeed, I find that I'm the one with the extra work of correcting other people's errors in work that affects us all.

But you know what? My willingness to set things right is under my control, and the truth is that other people are not responsible for living up to my, or your, standards. If other people don't meet our expectations, we can change our expectations rather than banish that person from our lives. We all can, should, and do draw some uncrossable lines, but we need to remember that it takes a lot of energy to maintain those boundaries, and that's energy we don't have available for anything else. We don't (I hope!) value friendships in terms of money, but we can budget our energy priorities, and not waste our energy (or give up our personal power, if you want to think of it another way) on "the small stuff." Perfect trust is about perceiving limits, and exploring our own options within them as much as it is about holding other people to our standards.

Perfect trust involves us in another way, too. When someone betrays our trust, our obligation is to learn from the experience. I don't mean learn how to get even, but learn how to see it coming next time, learn how to duck without losing our balance, learn how to shift our own way of looking at thing so we don't end up giving our power to the person who "dissed" us. Holding a grudge, never forgetting an insult to our honor, waiting for the other person to realize the error of their ways and apologize, these are ways we cede our personal power to that other person.

The energy we put into our "righteousness" is energy we could be using to play with our kids or volunteer at the food bank or write the great American novel!

Perfect love and perfect trust isn't about rose gardens and not having to worry about anything. It's not even all that much about other people's behavior and responsibility. It's about seeing the world in a way that lets us stay in control of our personal power. Put another way, it's about making sure that what we do (what we say, think, and how we act and feel) attunes us to or keeps us in attunement with our true (an ye harm none, do as ye) will.

If we say that we can't circle with So-and-So ever again, then we're giving So-and-So control over where and when we circle! All s/he has to do is show up, and we're outta there, no matter how much we wanted to be part of the event. If we're among the officiating Circle, we've set ourselves a really distracting problem (unless we're allowing ourselves to be so isolated from our community that we don't participate at all, on the off chance *that person* will be there.

I had that choice to make once: I had loved and trusted someone imperfectly (unrealistically, beyond her capacity to meet my expectations) and got burned pretty badly. Like most people are in such circumstances, I was reluctant for a number of reasons to be anywhere she might be. I dreaded even meeting her again, but I dreaded even more the prospect of giving her the power to decide where and when I could be part of our community. (As it happens, I stayed, and she left. I wasn't the only person she'd disappointed, and she herself was the person she most significantly betrayed.)

That's how I answered the question of what was more important, my grudge, my sense of betrayal, my insecurity and discomfort, or my participation in the life of the local community and my continuing spiritual growth. But there's an even more important question to ask, or maybe just a more direct way of asking the same one. What's more important, your ego or your relationship with/promises to the God/dess? Can we really think that the God/dess needs us to "defend" her by refusing to speak to or circle with somebody who has offended us? Can we really think that a serious offense is properly dealt with in junior-high "s/he's not my friend anymore" mode? Do we really honor the God/dess or our beliefs or our Oaths or Degrees, or even our obligations to community, by taking such an attitude?

Let me say that I don't hold myself up as a perfect example of perfect love and perfect trust. Often enough I've had to rely on my friends and colleagues to tap me on the shoulder and raise their eyebrows to me when I'm acting like a cranky toddler. But we need to be perfectly loving and trusting of ourselves, too. There are times when I feel unlovable, when I've been deliberately rude or failed to consider there might be a legitimate excuse for someone else's behavior, and I don't mind admitting it because I know you'll be nodding in agreement that you've done the same thing. If my trust that you're going to be doing your best and striving to do better is to have any meaning, then I have to extend it to myself, too, and believe that, even though we all make mistakes sometimes, it's still consistent with our true wills to love and trust each other, to desire and intend the best for each other and ourselves, and trust that we are all worthy of the God/dess' love.

That's my perspective on perfect love and perfect trust. At the entrance to an Initiatory Circle, the question is whether we have the courage to make the assay; "perfect love and perfect trust" are passwords by which we indicate our commitment to those acts of will, not the qualities we're looking for in a vacation experience.

Bibliography

Adler, Margot, *Drawing Down the Moon*. Boston: Beacon Press, 1979.

Amber K., *Covencraft, Witchcraft for Three or More*. St. Paul: Llewellyn Worldwide, 1998.

April. *Divine Sorrow, Divine Gift.* Unpublished book, 2005.

Boston Women's Health Collective, Inc., *Our Bodies, Ourselves*. New York: Simon & Schuster, 1973.

———. *Ourselves and Our Children*. New York: Random House, 1978.

Bonewits, Isaac, *Witchcraft: a Concise Guide*. Miami, Florida: Earth Religions Press, 1971, 2001.

Bosworth, Joseph, and T. Northcote Toller, *An Anglo-Saxon Dictionary*. London: Oxford University Press, 1964.

Bradshaw, John, *Homecoming, Reclaiming and Championing Your Inner Child*. New York, Bantam Books, 1990.

Buckland, Raymond, *Buckland's Complete Book of Witchcraft*. St. Paul: Llewellyn Publications, 1986.

Budapest, Zsuzsanna. *The Holy Book of Women's Mysteries complete in one volume*. Berkeley: Wingbow Press, 1980, 1989.

Campbell, Joseph. *Historical Atlas of World Mythology*. New York: Perrenial Library, Harper and Row, 1988.

Capra, Fritjof. *The Tao of Physics*. New York: Bantam Books, 1984.

Castaneda, Carlos. *Teachings of Don Juan: a Yaqui Way of Knowledge*. Berkeley: University of California Press, 1968.

Crowley, Vivienne. *Wicca: The Old Religion in the New Age*. Wellingborough, Northamptonshire, England: The Aquarian Press, 1989.

Cunningham, Scott. *Wicca: a Guide for the Solitary Practitioner*. St. Paul: Llewellyn Publications, 1989.

———— and David Harrington. *The Magical Household*, St. Paul, Llewellyn Publications, 1989.

————. *The Magic in Food*. St. Paul: Llewellyn Publications, 1991.

————. *The Truth About Witchcraft Today*. St. Paul: Llewellyn Publications, 1988.

Dreikurs, Rudolf, M.D. with Vicki Soltz, R.N. *Children: the Challenge*. New York: E.P. Dutton, 1964, 1987.

Farrar, Janet and Stewart. *A Witches Bible Compleat*, combined volumes I and II. New York: Magickal Child Publishing, 1981, 1984.

Forward, Susan, and Craig Buck. *Toxic Parents*. New York, Bantam Books, 1989.

Grey Cat. *Advancing Skills and Knowledge: Deepening Witchcraft*. Toronto: ECW Press, 2002.

Hawking, Stephen W. *A Brief History of Time*. New York: Bantam Books, 1988.

Hutton, Ronald. *The Triumph of the Moon*. Oxford: Oxford University Press, 1999.

Kübler-Ross, Elisabeth. *On Death and Dying*. New York McMillan, 1970.

Monks of New Skete. *In the Spirit of Happiness*. Boston: New York, London, Little, Brown and Company, 1999.

Moody, Raymond A., Jr., M.D. *Life After Life*. New York: Bantam Books, 1977.

O'Gaea, Ashleen. *Raising Witches: Teaching the Wiccan Faith to Children*. Franklin Lakes, New Jersey: New Page Books, 2002.

————. *In the Service of Life: a Wiccan Perspective on Death*. New York: Kensington Press, 2003.

————. *Celebrating the Seasons of Life: Samhain to Ostara*. Franklin Lakes, New Jersey: New Page Books, 2004.

————. *Celebrating the Seasons of Life: Beltane to Mabon*. Franklin Lakes: New Page Books, 2004.

Potts, Billie. *Witches Heal*. Ann Arbor, Michigan: DuReve Publications, 1988.

Samuels, L.T., *The Everything Kids' Witches and Wizards Book*. Avon, Massachusetts: Adams Media Corporation, 2000.

Smith, Lendon H., M.D. *The Children's Doctor*. Englewood Cliffs, New Jersey: Prentice Hall, Inc., 1969.

————. *Improving Your Child's Behavior Chemistry*. New York: Pocket Books, 1976.

Sousa, Mrs. Marion. *Childbirth at Home*. New York: Bantam Books, 1977.

Starhawk, Diane Baker, and Anne Hill. *Circle Round, Raising Children in Goddess Traditions*. New York: Bantam Books, 1998.

————. M. Macha Nightmare & the Reclaiming Collective. *The Pagan Book of Living and Dying*. San Francisco: HarperSanFrancisco, 1997.

————. *The Spiral Dance, a Rebirth of the Ancient Religion of the Great Goddess*. San Francisco: Harper & Row Publishers, 1979, 1989.

Stone, Merlin. *When God Was a Woman*. San Diego: New York, London: Harcourt, Brace, Jovanovich, 1976.

Tolkien, J.R.R. *The Hobbit*. New York: Ballantine Books, 1986.

———. *The Lord of the Rings*. New York: Ballantine Books, 1971.

Index

About the Author

Ashleen O'Gaea, a Third-Degree Wiccan, was in 1988 among the founding members of TAWN, the Tucson, Arizona Area Wiccan-Pagan Network. With her husband/high priest Canyondancer, she established the Adventure Tradition of Wicca in 1989, and led its first coven, Campsight, from its foundation in 1991 until its amicable dissolution in 2004. In 2000, O'Gaea was a cofounder of Mother Earth Ministries-ATC, a Neo-Pagan prison ministry for which she answers inmate letters from all over the U.S. Ordained by the Aquarian Tabernacle Church in June of 2004, O'Gaea is the author of several articles and books about Wicca. She lives with Canyondancer at the Adventure Traditionstead with a silly old dog and three affectionate cats.